In this WMG Writer's Guide, *USA Today* bestselling author and former publisher Dean Wesley Smith addresses the ten most damaging myths that writers believe in modern publishing.

The
WMG Writer's Guide
Series

*Think Like a Publisher 2014: A Step-By-Step Guide
to Publishing Your Own Books*

Killing the Top Ten Sacred Cows of Publishing

*Deal Breakers 2013:
Contract Terms Writers Should Avoid*

*The Pursuit of Perfection:
And How It Harms Writers*

*Surviving the Transition: How Writers Can Thrive
in the New World of Publishing*

KILLING
THE TOP 10
Sacred Cows
OF PUBLISHING

A WMG WRITER'S GUIDE

DEAN WESLEY SMITH

WMG PUBLISHING

Killing the Top Ten Sacred Cows of Publishing

Published 2014 by WMG Publishing
www.wmgpublishing.com
Cover art © copyright Robyn Mackenzie/Dreamstime
Book and cover design copyright © 2014 WMG Publishing
Cover design by Allyson Longueira/WMG Publishing
ISBN-13: 978-0-615-95951-1
ISBN-10: 0-615-95951-2

First published in slightly different form on Dean Wesley Smith's blog at www.deanwesleysmith.com in 2013.

Contents

Introduction 1

Sacred Cow #1: 5
There Is Only One Right Way to Do Anything in Publishing

Sacred Cow #2: 17
Writing Fast Is Bad

Sacred Cow #3: 27
You Must Rewrite to Make Something Good

Sacred Cow #4: 41
You Must Have an Agent to Sell a Book

Sacred Cow #5: 53
Books Are Events

Sacred Cow #6: 63
Selling a Novel to Traditional Publishing Will Guarantee the Novel Is Quality; Or Conversely, Not Selling a Novel to Traditional Publishing Will Mean the Novel Is Not Quality

Sacred Cow #7: 75
To Sell Either to Editors or Readers, You Must Write What Is Hot

Sacred Cow #8: 83
You Can't Make a Living with Your Fiction

Sacred Cow #9: 95
To Be Good, Writing Must Be Hard

Sacred Cow #10: 105
If I Do (This or That), I Will Kill My Career

About the Author 115

KILLING
THE TOP 10
Sacred Cows
OF PUBLISHING

A WMG WRITER'S GUIDE

INTRODUCTION

In 2010 I started doing short blog posts about the myths that hurt fiction writers that I had seen over my forty years in publishing. I honestly have no idea why I started these articles, but right from the start I called the myths of publishing "Sacred Cows."

Over the next few years I wrote upwards of 50 "Sacred Cows" knocking down one myth or another, or at least attempting to. And then two years ago I went back and updated some of the myths as indie publishing started to take hold.

Then, over the last two months of 2013, I updated these ten again, picking what I thought were the ten most damaging myths that writers believe in modern publishing.

An Important Note About This Book

In this book, I am only talking about commercial fiction. Nonfiction often has similar problems, and fiction written as a hobby has yet a different set of problems and myths.

But for this book, I am talking to writers who want to make a living with their fiction and sell a lot of copies, either through traditional publishers or through their own indie press.

So Who Am I to Try to Kill These Myths?

I think at one point or another since 1974, I fell into one or more of these myths, sometimes more than one at a time. Before I fell for the rewriting and writing slow myth, I wrote and sold two short stories and a lot of poetry in 1974 and 1975. Then I went down into the myths taught by college classes and didn't sell a thing for the next seven years.

Once I finally got out of those myths in 1982, I sold professionally over 200 short stories and wrote far more, and I have sold traditionally over 100 novels and written even more. I am considered one of the most prolific authors working at the moment.

During the years I was also an editor, starting as the first reader and publisher for Pulphouse Publishing in 1987, then staying a publisher as well as editing some lines for Pulphouse. I also helped my wife, Kristine Kathryn Rusch, at times as a first reader for *The Magazine of Fantasy and Science Fiction.*

In 1995 I started an almost three-year run as the fiction editor for *VB Tech Magazine.* Then in the late 1990s I also went to work for Pocket Books as the fiction editor for *Star Trek: Strange New Worlds.* I did that for ten years. Now I am one of the executive editors for *Fiction River* and often edit a volume myself. I was nominated five times for the Hugo Award for my editing.

And during all those years being a publisher and editor, I got to talk a lot with writers coming into the business. And all of them were dealing with one myth or another. Often a myth had them stopped cold.

In the late 1990s, Kris and I also started to teach, trying to help professional writers who were stuck to move forward in their careers. We've been doing that, as well as teaching online, since. Many, many of the writers we've helped were stuck in the myths.

So I hope this book helps you with your writing. I'll be happy to answer questions on my website at www.deanwesleysmith.com. And I am writing more Killing the Sacred Cows chapters there, so stop by and join in the fun.

Two Important Points

I will repeat this over and over throughout this book. But I want to be clear right up front here.

1) Every writer is different.

2) And if you can't enjoy your writing, what is the point?

Now off into the myths of fiction writing. There are a lot of them.

In this book I've tried to take a pretty good shot at the top ten. Enjoy.

—*Dean Wesley Smith*
January 5, 2014
Lincoln City, Oregon

Sacred Cow #1

THERE IS ONLY ONE RIGHT WAY TO DO ANYTHING IN PUBLISHING

That is the only way to do it."

How often do writers in this business hear that phrase? Some writer or editor or agent telling the young writer to do something as if that something was set in stone. Nope.

The truth is that nothing in this business is set in stone. *Nothing.*

And everything is changing so fast, what might have been true three years ago is very bad advice now.

For example, three years or so ago a wonderful new professional writer in one of the workshops here e-mailed a well-written query with ten sample pages and a synopsis of the novel off to an editor in New York from the workshop. The next morning she came out of her room smiling. Overnight, the editor had asked to see the entire book. So being am imp, I went to that publisher's website and printed off the guidelines, which said

5

in huge letters "*No electronic submissions and absolutely no un-agented submissions.*"

Lucky for her she hadn't bothered to look at the guidelines, or listen to all the people who said she needed an agent, or believed there was only one way to get her book read at that company.

Now, I would have asked her why she bothered even going to a traditional publisher.

Nothing in this business is set in stone. Nothing.

Of course, that little story about not looking at guidelines will cause massive anger to come at me I'm sure.

As will my question as to why she even bothered with a traditional publisher.

So before you go tossing bricks at my house because you need a rule to follow, let me back up and try to explain what I am saying here. And what I will be saying throughout this book. Then you can toss the brick.

All Writers Are Different

Perfectly good advice for one writer will be flat wrong for the writer standing beside him.

Some writers feel for some reason that they need an agent. Some writers need the control of indie publishing, but for some other writer that control would scare them to death. Some writers know business, other writers need help figuring out how to balance a checkbook and wouldn't understand cash flow in a flood of money.

So how do writers learn? And how can those of us who have walked this publishing road help out the newer professionals coming in? **Carefully** is my answer. But now let me try to expand on that.

How do writers learn?

1) Take every statement by any **WRITER**, including me, with your bull detector turned on. If it doesn't sound right for some reason, ignore it. It may be right for the writer speaking and wrong for you. And for heaven's sake, be extra, extra careful when you listen to any writer who is not a long distance down the publishing road ahead of you. Some of the stupidest advice I have ever heard has come from writers with three or four short story sales talking on some convention panel like they understand the publishing business and think that everything they say is a rule.

In fact, I get that all the time in e-mail. Honestly. Some beginning writer with a couple novels published is insistent that I am doing something wrong. I might be and I always keep an open mind and look at what they are saying. But most of the time it's the writer telling me in no uncertain terms I need an agent or need to publish in traditional publishing as they did. (I guess they forgot to look at my bio with over a hundred traditionally published novels behind me.)

So, when some advice doesn't feel right, check in with yourself and ask yourself where the concern is coming from. Is the concern that some advice isn't right in conflict with something you learned in school from someone who wasn't a writer? Or does the advice just not feel right for you. Check in with yourself on each thing you hear.

2) Take any statement by any **EDITOR** and run it through a very fine filter. Ask yourself why they are saying what they are saying, what corporate purpose does it fill, and can you use it to help you?

Remember, editors are not writers.

And they only know what they need in their one publishing house. Editors have the best of intentions to help writers.

Honest, they do. But they often do not understand how writers make money, and most think that writers can't make a living, since all they see are the small advances to writers they are paying. Just nod nicely when they start into that kind of stuff and move on.

And remember, they always have a corporate agenda. It's the nature of their job and who they work for.

3) Take any statement from an **AGENT** with a giant salt-shaker full of salt, then bury it with more salt. Then just ignore it. Agents are not writers; agents can't help you rewrite, and they only know about six or seven editors and nothing at all about the new world of indie publishing.

In this modern world, agents work for publishers, not you. If any agent is flat telling you that you must do something, and it sounds completely wrong to you, my suggestion to you is RUN! Remember, agents have an agenda. It is not your agenda. It is their agenda.

The day of agents in publishing is dropping away, finally. They are working for publishers or becoming publishers. So be careful when listening to what they are saying. There are many alternatives to needing an agent in this new world.

So how do writers learn?

—By going to lots and lots of conferences and listening to hundreds of writers and editors and taking only the information that seems right to you. This takes years. Think of it like going to college for four years. And after that the learning never stops.

—Read lots and lots of books by writers and only take what seems right for you.

—Read and follow lots of different publishing blogs, from publishersmarketplace.com to thepassivevoice.com to writer blogs like Kristine Kathryn Rusch's blog and Joe Konrath's blog. And then only take what information seems right to you.

—Learn business, basic business, and apply that to writing as well. Writing is a business, a very big business. Keep learning business and contracts and copyright as you go along.

—And keep writing and practicing and getting your work out to readers to get reader feedback.

How Can Professional Writers Help Newer Writers?

1) Professional writers, keep firmly in mind that your way, the way you broke in might be wrong for just about everyone else in the room listening to you. Especially today, when the world of publishing is shifting so fast it's hard for anyone to keep up. A story about your first sale in 1992 as a way to do it just won't be relevant in any real way to a new writer in 2014. Be clear that you understand that.

And remember, slush piles are gone. Writers are going directly to readers these days more and more. And then editors find them and make them offers.

And remember, the contracts you saw in 1990 and 2000 don't exist these days. Advances are much, much smaller and terms much, much worse. Don't give contract advice unless you see the contract and understand what the young writers are seeing. You will be stunned at what publishers are offering young writers these days.

2) Keep abreast of what the newer writers are facing. I get angry at times because newer writers keep accusing me of having some advantage. I don't, really. I have years more of practice, sure, and I have more work in inventory, and I understand business better than most, and I have a better work ethic than most writers on the planet.

But even with all that, I still have to get my work to readers in some fashion just as everyone else.

There is no secret road to selling to readers (or editors) just because you have done it before. I wish like hell there was, but alas, if it exists, I haven't found the entrance ramp yet. So to help myself, I keep abreast of what newer writers are facing, I help teach them how to get through the starting gate and become better storytellers, so I also know how to do it with my work. Duh. I learn from newer writers as I teach them.

3) **Stay informed as to the changes in publishing and don't be afraid of the new technology.**

Bragging that you belong to the Church of Luddite or that you won't touch any Apple product or that you hate smartphones sure won't instill a lot of confidence in the newer writers who live with this modern publishing world and use the new technology. And wishing things would go back to the way they were just doesn't help either.

And for heaven's sake, understand sampling and indie publishing and cover design and blurb writing and apps and all the basic skills needed by writers these days.

Newer Writers Need Set Rules

Writers, especially newer writers are hungry for set rules.

This business is fluid and crazy most of the time, and the need for security screams out in most of us. So in the early years we writers search for "rules" to follow, shortcuts that will cut down the time involved, secret handshakes that will get us through doors. It is only after a lot of time that professional writers come to realize that the only rules are the ones we put on ourselves. In my early years I was no different.

Writers are people who sit alone in a room and make stuff up. The problem we have is that when we get insecure without rules, we make stuff up as well.

When we don't understand something, we make something up to explain it. Then when someone comes along with a "this is how you do it" stated like a rule, you jump to the rule like a drowning man reaching for a rope. And when someone else says "Let go of the rope to make it to safety," you get angry and won't let go of that first safety line.

In all these chapters, that's what I will be trying to tell you to do: **Let go of the rope and trust your own talents and knowledge.**

When I first wrote these chapters online over almost three years ago, my suggestions caused some very "interesting" letters from writers mad at me for challenging their lifeline rules.

The desire for safety and rules is one of the reasons that so many myths have grown up in this business.

Rule upon rule upon rule, all imposed from the outside. Most are just bad advice believed by the person giving the advice at the time.

The key is to let go of the rope, swim on your own, and find out what works for you.

If you believe you must rewrite, write a couple dozen stories and get them out to readers without rewrites to see what happens. If you are having no luck finding an agent, send it to editors instead. Or better yet, indie publish it.

If you think you can't write more than 500 words a day, push a few days to double or triple that and see what happens. Push and experiment and find out what is right for you.

Will it scare you? Yes. But I sure don't remember anyone telling me this profession was easy or not scary. Those two things are not myths just yet.

Okay, all that said, here are a few major areas where following rules blindly can be dangerous to writers. I will talk about these in coming chapters. But for the moment, I want to touch on them right here because they are major.

1) "You must rewrite."

This is just silly, since writing comes out of the creative side of our brains and rewriting comes from the critical learned side.

Creative side is always a better writer. But again, this is different for every writer no matter what level. Some writers never rewrite other than to fix a few typos, others do a dozen drafts, and both sell. Those professionals have figured out what is best for them. But if a younger writer listens to someone who says you MUST rewrite everything, it could kill that writer's voice. This rule is just flat destructive. Keep your guard up on this one. Experiment on both sides and then do what works for you, what sells for you.

2) "You must have an agent."

This is such bad advice for such a large share of writers these days, it's scary.

These days there are many ways of not using or needing an agent.

—Using an intellectual copyright attorney is one way. Cheap and you don't have to pay them 15% of everything.

—Doing it yourself is fine as well.

—Indie publish it and let editors come to you.

3) "Editors don't like (blank) so you shouldn't write that way."

I can't begin to tell you how many thousand times I have answered questions like "Can I write in first person? Editor's don't like that." No rules, just write your own story with passion and then figure out a path to get it to readers.

If the readers don't like it, they simply won't buy it. No big deal. Stop worrying about what editors or agents want and write what you want. And then let readers decide.

Be an artist. Protect your work and don't let anyone in the middle of it.

Think for yourself, be yourself, write your own stuff. No rules.

4) "It's a tight market so you need to do (blank)." or "I need to figure out a way to get my fiction noticed in the noise."

You want a secret? It's always been a tight market and there has always been noise.

Right now there are more books being published every year than ever before, more markets, more ways for writers to make money. This silly "tight market" statement always sounds so full of authority coming from some young agent or editor. And it will drive a new writer into doing a dozen rewrites on a novel for someone who really doesn't know what they are talking about and couldn't write a novel themselves if forced to at gunpoint.

Again, my suggestion is stop letting others into your work and get it to readers. Let readers find it.

Truth: Publishing and readers are always looking for good books and new writers. And it has always been tight in one way or another. And there has always been noise.

Focus on what you can control such as how much you write, the quality of your own work, and where and how you get it to the most readers.

A Brand New World

Right now publishing is going through some major changes, all rotating around distribution for the most part. Writers have been so shut out with the system in New York that they are turning more and more to taking control of various aspects of their own work with indie publishing. POD and electronic publishing is allowing authors to become both writer and publisher and electronic distribution is allowing readers to find more work from their favorite writers, often either new work, dangerous work, or work long out of print..

This new area of publishing is quickly becoming full of "rules" and future myths. For the longest time publishing your own work was looked down on by "the ruling class" (whoever they are). Now, except for a few holdouts in the basements of the

Church of Luddite, writers are taking the new technologies and running with them.

Common sense: It takes a lot of practice to become a professional-level storyteller. You may think your first story or novel is brilliant because you rewrote it ten times and your workshop loved it, but alas, it might not be. In this new market, just as in the old one, the readers will judge. Let them, either through traditional channels or indie publishing. And then write the next book and the next and keep working to become better. Keep writing and learning.

It's called "practice" which is a term most writers hate.

Now I'm Taking the Rope Away

As I said above, writers tend to have this fantastic need for rules. We all want to make some sort of order out of this huge business. And actually, there is order if you know where to look and how to look. So instead of giving you rules, let me help you find order without myths and rules.

1) Publishing is a business. A large business run by large corporations in traditional publishing or your own home business when you are indie publishing. But it is always a business. If you remember that, learn basic business, understand corporation politics and thinking, learn copyrights, most everything that happens anywhere, from bookstores to distributors to traditional publishers, will make some sort of sense. Don't take anything personally. It's just business and that is the truth.

2) All writers write differently. And that includes you. My way of producing words won't be correct for anyone but me. So instead of listening to others looking for the secret, just go home, sit down at your writing computer, and experiment with every different form and method until you find the way that produces selling fiction that readers like and buy. Find your own way to produce words that sell.

3) Learning and continuing to learn is critical. This business keeps changing and the only way to stay abreast of the changes is to go out and keep learning and talk with other writers and find advice that makes sense to you and your way. Go to workshops, conferences, conventions and anything else you can find to get bits of learning. Read everything you can find about the business and the craft of telling great stories.

My goal has always been to learn one thing new every week (at least). I've been doing that since my early days and it has worked for me, and kept me focused on learning. Find what works for you.

I know those three things don't seem to give you any secrets, don't really show you the path to selling and getting readers to really want your work. But actually, they do. And if you just keep them in mind and don't allow yourself to get caught in strange rules and myths, you will move faster toward your goal, whatever that goal in writing may be.

It's your writing. It's your art. Stop looking for the secrets and stand up for your work.

Trust your own voice, your own methods of working. Get your work to editors who will buy it. Or indie publish it and let readers buy it. Or both.

And if your methods are not producing selling work that readers love, try something new.

Keep learning. Keep practicing your art.

The only right way in this business is your way.

Sacred Cow #2

WRITING FAST IS BAD

Or said in myth fashion: **WRITING SLOW EQUALS WRITING WELL.** Or the flip side: **WRITING FAST EQUALS WRITING POORLY.**

This comes out of everyone's mouth at one point or another in a form of apology for our work. "Oh, I just cranked that off."

Or the flip side... "This is some of my best work. I've been writing it for over a year."

Now this silly idea that the writing process has anything at all to do with quality of the work has been around in publishing for just over 100 years now, pushed mostly by the literature side and the college professors.

It has no basis in any real fact when it comes to writers. **None.** If you don't believe me, start researching how fast some of the classics of literature were written.

But don't ask major professional writers out in public. Remember we know this myth and lie about how really hard we do work. (Yup, that's right, someone who makes stuff up for a living will lie to you. Go figure.) So you have to get a long-term professional writer in a private setting. Then maybe with a few drinks under his belt the pro will tell you the truth about any project.

In my Writing in Public posts this year, I am doing my best to knock some of this myth down and just show what a normal day in a life can produce, even with me doing a bunch of other things at the same time.

My position:

NO WRITER IS THE SAME. NO PROJECT IS THE SAME.

And put simply:

THE QUALITY OF THE FINAL PRODUCT HAS NO RELATIONSHIP TO THE SPEED, METHOD, OR FEELING OF THE WRITER WHILE WRITING.

That's right, one day I could write some pages feeling sick, almost too tired to care, where every word is a pain, and the next day I write a few more pages feeling good and the words flowing freely and a week later I won't be able to tell which day was which from the writing.

How I feel when I write makes no difference to the quality of what I produce. None. Damn it, it should, but it just doesn't.

And I just laugh when a myth like this one attempts to lump all writers into the same boat and make us all write exactly the same way book after book after book.

No writer works the same, even from book to book or short story to short story.

In fact, as you will discover watching me over this year of writing in public, I don't do any story or novel similar to any other.

Talk to any writer, and I mean privately, and you will discover that one of the writer's books was written quickly, maybe even in a few weeks, while another book took the writer a half year to finish and he was deathly ill during half the writing time. And you, as a reader, reading the two books, would never be able to tell the difference.

But yet, traditional publishing, college professors, and just about anyone who even thinks about the writer behind the words has a belief system that words must be struggled over to be good.

Well, yes, sometimes.

And sometimes not.

Sometimes a writer gets into a white-hot heat and a book flows faster than the writer can type, getting done in just a number of days or weeks. And sometimes it just doesn't work that way.

Sometimes a writer has a deadline to hit and pushes to hit it, spending more hours in the chair, thus calling it writing fast. Some writers think and research a book for a few months, then write it in a few weeks. Some writers spend a month or two on a detailed outline, then take a month to actually write the book. Some writers start with a title, some write chapters out of order and then put it all together like a puzzle.

And on and on and on.

Every writer is different. Every writer's method is different *There is no correct, mandated way to write a book. Just your way.*

The Myth of Writing Slow to Write Better Actually Hurts Writers

There are two sides of our brains. The creative side and the critical side.

The creative side has been taking in stories since the writer started reading, knowing how to put words together at a deep level. The critical side lags far, far behind the creative side, learning rules that some English teacher or parent forced into the critical mind.

The creative side is always a much better writer than the critical side. Always. It never switches, no matter how long you write.

Long-term (20 years and up) professional writers have learned to trust that creative side and we tend to not mess much with what it creates for us. Of course, this lesson for most of us was learned the hard way, but that's another long chapter for another book.

A new writer who believes the myth that all good fiction must be written slowly and labor-intensive (called work) suddenly one day finds that they have written a thousand words in 35 minutes. The new writer automatically thinks, "Oh, my, that has to be crap. I had better rewrite it."

What has just happened is that the wonderful writing the creative side of the mind has just produced is then killed by the critical side, dumbed down, voice taken out, anything good and interesting removed.

All caused by this myth.

And professional editors in New York are no better, sadly. I once got a rewrite request on a major book from my editor. I agreed with about nine-tenths of the suggestions, so I spent the next day rewriting the book, fixing the problems, and was about to send the manuscript back when Kris stopped me.

The conversation went something like this:

"Don't send it, sit on it a few weeks," Kris said, looking firm and intense, as only Kris can look.

"Why not?" I asked, not remembering at that moment that the myth was a major part of traditional publishing.

"The editor will think you didn't work on it and that it is crap," Kris said.

"But I agreed and fixed everything," I said, starting to catch a clue, but not yet willing to admit defeat.

Kris just gave me that "stare" and I wilted, knowing she was completely correct.

I held the rewrite for three weeks, sent it back with a letter praising the rewrite comments and a slight side comment about how hard I had worked on them, even though I wrote most of another book in the period of time I was holding the rewrite. Story ended happily, editor was happy and commented on how fast I managed to get the rewrites done, all because Kris remembered the myth and how it functions.

Now, let me do something that just annoys people. I'm going to do the math.

The Math of Writing Fast

This chapter when finished is going to be around 2,000 words. That is about 8 manuscript pages with each page averaging 250 words per page.

So say I wrote only 250 words, one manuscript page per day on a new novel.

It takes me about 15 minutes, give-or-take (depending on the book and the day and how I'm feeling) to write 250 words of fiction. (Each writer is different. Time yourself.)

So if I spent that 15 minutes per day writing on a novel, every day for one year, I would finish a 90,000-plus word novel, a large paperback book, in 365 days.

I would be a one-book-per-year writer, pretty standard in science fiction and a few other genres.

15 minutes per day equals one novel per year.

Oh, my, if I worked really, really hard and managed to get 30 minutes of writing in per day, I could finish two novels in a year.

And at that speed I would be considered fast. Not that I typed or wrote fast, just that I spent more time writing.

God forbid I actually write four pages a day, spend an entire hour per day sitting in a chair! I would finish four novels a year. At that point I would be praised in the romance genre and called a hack in other genres.

See why I laugh to myself when some writer tells me they have been working really, really hard on a book and it took them a year to write? What did they do for 23 hours and 45 minutes every day?

The problem is they are lost in the myth. Deep into the myth that writing must be work, that it must be hard, that you must "suffer for your art" and write slowly.

Bull-puckey. Writing is fun, easy, and enjoyable. If you want hard work, go dig a ditch for a water pipe on a golf course in a steady rain on a cold day. That's work. Sitting at a computer and making stuff up just isn't work. It's a dream job.

Spend More Time in the Chair

Oh, oh, I just gave you the secret to being a "fast" writer or a "prolific" writer. Just spend more time writing.

I am the world's worst typist. I use four fingers, up from two, and if I can manage 250 words in fifteen minutes I'm pretty happy. I tend to average around 750-1,000 words per hour of work. Then I take a break. I am not a "fast" typist, but I am considered a "fast" writer because I spend more time writing than the myth allows.

That's the second thing that makes this myth so damaging to writers. It doesn't allow writers to just spend more time practicing their art. In fact, the myth tells writers that if they do spend more time working to get better, they are worse because they produce more fiction.

Writing is the only art where spending less time practicing is considered a good thing.

In music we admire musicians who practice ten or more hours a day. Painters and other forms of artists are the same. Only in writing does the myth of not practicing to get better come roaring in.

We teach new writers to slow down, to not work to get better, to spend fewer and fewer hours at writing, to not practice, and then wonder why so many writers don't make it to a professional level.

We No Longer Have to Wait for Traditional Publishers

For the last few decades, unless a writer wrote under many pen names, we were forced by the market to write fewer books per year. But now, with indie publishing, we can once again write as much as we want.

And we can write anything we want.

We can sell some books to traditional publishers, we can indie publish other books and stories. Or as I am doing, we can create our own market and indie publish almost everything.

The new world has lifted the market restrictions on speed of writing. Now those of us who actually want to sit and write for more than 15 minutes per day can publish what we write in one way or another.

And being fast, meaning spending more time writing, is a huge plus with indie publishing. We are in a new golden age of fiction, especially short fiction, and just as in the first golden age, writing fast (meaning spending more time at your art) will be a good thing also for your pocketbook.

Writing Slow Equals Writing Better is a complete myth, a nasty sacred cow of publishing that hurts and stops writers who believe it.

—The truth is that no two writers work the same and no book is the same as the previous book or the next book.

—The truth is that writing fast is nothing more than spending more time every day writing.

—The truth is that there should be no rule about speed relating to quality.

—The truth is there should be no rule that lumps all writers into one big class. There should only be your way of writing.

Be Careful!

Sadly, this myth is firm in the business, so writers who spend more time in the chair and who write more hours have to learn to work around the myth. We must learn to play the game that teachers, editors, book reviewers, and fans want us to play.

And if you decide you can spend more hours every day writing and working on your art, be prepared to face those who want you to write the way they do. Be prepared to face those who want to control your work. Be prepared to face criticism from failed writers (reviewers) who can't even manage a page a day, let alone more.

This speed myth is the worst myth of an entire book full of myths. Caution.

The best thing you can do is just keep your speed and your writing methods to yourself. Don't write in public as I am doing. You're an artist. Respect your way of doing things and just don't mention them to anyone.

Also, I beg of you that if you believe in the myth, please don't do the math about my age. I sold my first novel when I was 38 and have published over 100 novels. At one book per year, I must be at least 138 years old.

After my hard, single-page-of-writing every day, I sometimes feel that way.

Yeah, right.

But I stand by that story except when I am writing in public on my blog. (grin)

Sacred Cow #3

YOU MUST REWRITE
TO MAKE SOMETHING GOOD

That's one of the great myths of publishing. And one of the worst and most destructive to fiction writers.

First off, I want to repeat clearly what I said in the previous two chapters in different ways:

No writer is the same.

Let me repeat that with a few more words.

No writer works or thinks the same way, and there is no right way to work. Just your way.

That includes speed of writing, style of writing, and most importantly, how you handle rewrites of what you have written.

So, to make sure we are all speaking the same language, let me define a few terms that Kristine Kathryn Rusch and I have used for a long time now, and I will try to use in this discussion.

REDRAFT: That's when you take the typing you have done and toss it away, then write the story again from your memory of the idea. When you are redrafting, you are working from the creative side of your brain.

REWRITE: That's when you go into a manuscript after it is finished **in critical voice** and start changing things, usually major things like plot points, character actions, style of sentences, and so on. When you rewrite like this, you are working from the critical side of your mind. This often comes from fear or from workshop advice.

TOUCH-UP DRAFT: When you run through a manuscript fixing small things, things you wrote in notes while writing, things your trusted first reader found. Often very small things or typos. This draft takes almost no time, often less than half a day for a full novel, sometimes only an hour or so.

SPELL-CHECKING DRAFT: Since so many of us work with our grammar-checkers and spell-checkers off, we need a spell-check draft, often done before the manuscript is given to a first reader. This often takes an hour or so for a full novel.

Now, let me say right up front here that I am a three-draft writer. Most long-term pros that I have talked to in private are "three-draft" writers. Not all, since we all work differently, but a vast majority of the ones I have talked to use a process very near mine.

My process:

First draft I do as quickly as I can, staying solidly as much as possible in my creative side, adding in things I think about as I go along, until I get to the end of the draft. Again, I try to write as fast as the project will allow since I have discovered a long time ago that if I just keep typing, the less chance I have to get in my own way and screw things up.

Second draft I spellcheck and then give to my trusted first reader.

Third draft I touch up all the things my first reader has found and then I mail the novel or story.

If my first reader hates the story, I toss the draft away and redraft completely.

That's my process. I am a three-draft writer. (Unless I need to redraft, then I am a six-draft writer.)

More Basic Information About Writers

There is a way of describing and dividing writers into two major camps. Taker-outers and putter-inners.

In other words, a taker-outer is a writer who over-writes the first time through, then goes back and takes things out.

As a putter-inner, I write thin (my poetry background still not leaving me alone) and then as I go along, I cycle back and add in more and then cycle again and add in more, *staying in creative voice,* just floating around in the manuscript as I go along. Some people of this type make notes as they go along and then go back in a touch-up draft and put stuff in.

Okay, so terms done, on to the major topic.

So, what's the great myth about rewriting?

First, our colleges and our training and New York editors and agents all think that rewriting can make something better.

Most of the time that is just wrong.

Flat wrong when it comes to fiction. It might be right with poetry, or non-fiction or essays, but with fiction, it can hurt you if you believe this completely and let it govern your process.

Secondly, it makes writers think there is only one "right" way of writing.

And that if you don't fit into that way and rewrite everything, you are doing something wrong. That kind of thinking kills more good writers' careers than I can imagine, and I can imagine a great deal. And I have watched firsthand it kill more writer's dreams than I want to remember.

All writers are different, so sometimes a writer works with a ton of rewrites. Sometimes a writer just does one draft.

A Wonderful Conversation with a Master

One fine evening I was having a conversation with Algis Budrys about rewriting and why so many new writers believed the myth. He shrugged and said, "They don't know any better and no one has the courage to tell them." So I asked him if he ever thought rewriting could fix a flawed story. His answer was clear and I remember it word-for-word to this day: *"No matter how many times you stir up a steaming pile of crap, it's still just a steaming pile of crap."*

If you ever worry about not "fixing" a story because you didn't rewrite it, just put that quote on your wall.

So, as an example, let's take some new writer hoping to write a book that will sell at some point. This new writer does the near-impossible for most new writers and actually finishes the book. That's a huge success, but instead of just sending the book off and starting on a second book, this poor new writer has bought into the myth that everything **MUST** be rewritten before it can be good. (It makes the new writer feel like a "real writer" if they rewrite because all "real writers" rewrite.)

All beginning fiction writers believe this myth, and you hear it in comments about their novel like "Oh, it's not very good yet. Oh, it needs to be polished. Oh, it was JUST a first draft and can't be any good."

I even hear that come out of some newer professional writer's mouths. I **never** hear it from long-term pros (over 20 plus years making a living).

Of course, for the beginning writer, the first book just isn't very good most of the time. Duh, it's a first novel. It might be great, but it also might be crap. (Let me refer you back to Algis Budrys' comment.) More than likely the first book is flawed beyond rescue, but the writer won't know that, and the first reader won't be able to help "fix" anything besides typos and grammar.

So, what is the new writer to do at this point with a finished novel?

Simple. Mail it to editors or indie publish it yourself.

That's right, I said, *"Mail it or publish it."*

Awkkk! Has Dean lost it?

I can just hear the voices in your heads screaming now...

"But, it's no good! It needs a rewrite! It might be a steaming pile of crap. I can't mail something that's flawed to an editor!"

Or you indie published writers are thinking...

"I can't publish a book that's flawed or readers will hate me!"

And thus the myth has a stranglehold on you.

The great thing about editors is that we can't remember bad stories. We just reject them and move on.

Most of us, over the years and decades, have bought so much, we have a hard time remembering everything and everyone we bought. So you have nothing to lose by mailing it and everything to gain, just in case it happens to be good enough to sell.

And if it isn't, **WE WON'T REMEMBER. Why? Because we didn't read it. Duh.**

And readers of indie published books have a wonderful thing called "sampling." And taste. If the book sucks, oh, trust me, no reader but your family will buy it. And at that point you don't have a "career" to kill anyway. (Future chapter on that myth.)

Just because the book is bad doesn't mean someone will come to your house and arrest you if you mail it or publish it. Editors do not talk about manuscripts that don't work and readers never buy or read them.

Honestly, no one can shoot you for publishing it.

So get past the fear and just mail it. Or publish it. You have nothing to lose and everything to gain. (What happens if it is wonderful and will make you a million?)

One true thing about writing that is a firm rule: **There is no perfect book.** (No matter what some reviewer wants to think.)

(Also, there is a very true saying about writers that I will deal with in another chapter. Writers are the worst judges of their own work. Why is that? Because, simply, we wrote it and we know what was supposed to be on the page. It might not be, but we think it is. We just can't tell. A future myth chapter.)

If You Don't Rewrite, How Can You Learn?

You have to write new material to learn. No one ever learned how to be a creative writer by rewriting. Only by writing.

So, after the story or book is in the mail or published, start writing the next story or book, go to workshops and writers' conferences to learn storytelling skills, learn business, and meet people.

Study how other writers do things.

But keep writing that second story or book.

And then repeat.

Trust me, the second one will be a lot better than the first one, especially if you just trust yourself and write it and don't fall into the myth of rewriting.

When the second one is done, go celebrate again, then fix the typos and such and mail it to an editor who might buy it or publish it yourself, and then start writing again.

A writer is a person who writes.

Rewriting Is Not Writing

Yeah, I know what your English Professor tried to tell you. But if your English Professor could make a living writing fiction, they would have been doing it.

Putting new and original words on a page is writing. Nothing more, and nothing less.

—Research is not writing.

—Rewriting is not writing.

—Talking to other writers is not writing.

And what you will discover that is amazing is that the more you write, the better your skills become. With each story, each novel, you are telling better and better stories.

It's called **"practice"** (but again, no writer likes to think about that evil word).

Well, if you want to be a professional fiction writer, it's time to bring the word "practice" into your speaking. On your next novel, make it a practice session for cliffhangers. Mail the novel and then work on practicing something different on the next story or novel. And so on.

Follow Heinlein's Business Rules

I believe that a writer is a person who writes. An author is a person who has written.

I want to always be a writer, so I have, since 1982, followed Robert Heinlein's business rules. And those rules have worked for many, many of us for decades and decades.

His rules go simply:

1) You must write.

2) You must finish what you write.

3) You must not rewrite unless to editorial demand.

4) You must mail your work to someone who can buy it.

5) You must keep the work in the mail until someone buys it.

Those rules do seem so simple, and yet are so hard to follow at times. They set out a simple practice schedule and a clear process of what to do with your practice sessions when finished. But for this chapter, note rule #3. Harlan Ellison added to rule #3. "You must not rewrite unless to editorial demand." *Harlan addition: And then only if you agree.*

And, of course, if you indie publish, substitute "publish" in #4 for "mail" and let reader's buy it. And then for #5 just keep it for sale.

Speaking of Harlan, many of you know that over the decades he has tried to prove this point (and many others) to people. He would go into a bookstore, have someone give him a title or idea, then on a *manual* typewriter, he would sit in the bookstore window and write a short story, taping the finished pages on the window for everyone to read.

He never rewrote any of those stories. He fixed a typo or two, but that's it. And many of those stories won major awards in both science fiction and mystery and many are now in college text books being studied by professors who tell their students they must rewrite. But Harlan wrote all first draft, written fast, sometimes in a window while people watched him type every word.

I know, I was going to publish a three-volume set of these award-winning stories written in public back when I was doing

Pulphouse Publishing. But alas, he was still writing them, a new one almost every other week at that point, and the book never got out before we shut down. He's done enough since then to fill two more books at least.

Every writer is different.

If you want more on Heinlein's Rules, I did an almost two hour lecture (15 videos) on how and why Heinlein's Rules work and how they worked for me over the decades. It's under the lecture series tab if interested.

So, How Come Rewriting Makes Stories Worse Instead of Better?

Back to understanding how the brain works.

The creative side, the deep part of our brain, has been taking in story, story structure, sentence structure, character voice, and everything else for a very long time, since each of us read our first book or had a book read to us. It's that place where our author voice comes from, where the really unique ideas come from.

The critical side of the brain is full of all the crap you learned in high school, everything your college teachers said, what your workshop said, and the myths you have bought into like a fish biting on a yummy worm. Your critical voice is also full of the fear that comes out in "I can't show this to friends." Or, "What would my mother think?" That is all critical side thinking that makes you take a great story and dumb it down.

In pure storytelling skill level, the critical side is far, far behind the creative side of your brain. And always will be.

So, on a scale of one-to-ten, with ten being the top, the creative skills of a new writer with very few stories under his belt, if left alone, will produce a story at about a six or seven. However, at that point the writer's critical skills are lagging far behind, so if written critically, a new writer would create a story about four on the scale. So take a well-written story that first draft was a seven on the scale, then let a new writer rewrite it and down the level comes to five or so.

I can't tell you how many times I have seen a great story ruined by a number of things associated with this myth.

For example, take a great story, run it through a workshop, then try to rewrite it to group think. Yow, does it become dull, just as anything done by committee is dull. (Workshop myth coming in a future chapter.)

I helped start and run a beginners workshop when I was first starting out. None of us had a clue, but we were all learning fast. I would write a story a week (all I could manage with three jobs at the time) and mail it, then turn it into my workshop for audience reaction.

That's right, I mailed it before I gave it to my workshop. Why? Because I had no intention of ever rewriting it. I followed Heinlein's Rules.

And I sold a few stories that the workshop said failed completely, which taught me a lot, actually. If I had listened to them, I never would have made some of those early sales.

If you would like to see a first draft of one of my early stories, pick up Volume #1 of *Writers of the Future*. I was in the middle of moving from Portland to the Oregon Coast , actually packing the truck, when my then-wife, Denie, asked me if I had the story done for *Writers of the Future* that Algis Budrys had told me was starting up. I said no, the mailing deadline was the next day and I didn't have time.

Thankfully, Denie insisted I go finish it while she packed. I didn't tell her that I hadn't even started it yet and had no idea what to write.

I put the typewriter (electric) on a partially dismantled desk on top of a large box, sat on the edge of the bed, and wrote the story from start to finish having no idea what I was writing or where the story was going. Three hours later I finished the story called "One Last Dance" and mailed it on a dinner break.

That's right, it was a first draft on a typewriter. No spell-checker, no first reader, nothing.

Algis Budrys and Jack Williamson loved it and put it into the first volume, and because of that story, I ended up meeting Kris a couple of years later after Denie and I had gone our own ways. I also got lots of wonderful trips and money and a great workshop from that three-hour draft. And now, twenty-nine years later the story is still in print and I'm still proud of it.

All because I had the courage to write and mail first draft. Because I followed Heinlein's Rules.

I trusted my creative skills, I trusted my voice, and I was lucky enough to have someone who gave me support at that point in the writing.

Another Example: Every year for years, editor Denise Little and I would prove that same point again to early career writers. We forced them to write a short story overnight to an anthology idea and deadline, and those quickly-written stories were always better than the ones the same writers wrote over weeks before the workshop. And many of those stories, first drafts, have been in published anthologies out of New York.

The problem was that even though Denise and I harped on that lesson for years, most of those writers would then just go home and right back to rewriting, making their stories worse. That's how powerful this myth is.

The creative side is just a better writer than the critical side, no matter what the critical side tries to tell you.

Remember, the critical side has a voice of restraint and worry. But the creative side, as Kris likes to say, is your two-year-old child. It has no voice of reason and no way to fight. But if you let the child just play and get out of its way and stop trying to put your mother's or father's or teacher's voice on everything it does, you will be amazed at what you create.

One More Point

Every writer is different, granted, but I have only met a few writers who really, really love to rewrite. Most find it horrid and a ton of work, but we all, with almost no exception, love to write original stuff.

If you can get past the myth of rewriting, writing becomes a lot more fun.

Following Heinlein's Rules is a ton of fun, actually. And you end up writing and selling a lot of stuff as well.

However, this myth is so deep, I imagine many of you are angry at me at this moment, and trust me, even if you get past this myth in private, out in public you will need to lie.

That's right, I just told a bunch of fiction writers to lie. Go figure.

Maybe you don't need to go as far as Hemingway and tell people that you must write standing up because writing comes from the groin or some such nonsense. (He loved screwing with new writers minds.) But you do need to hide your process.

I know one writer who at writers' conferences tells people with a straight face he does upwards of ten drafts. I knew better and one day, in private, I asked him why he said that.

He just shrugged. "I like making my audience happy, so I tell them what they want to believe about me. It makes them believe my books and stories are worth more if I tell them I rewrote them ten times."

In other words, even though the reality of professional fiction writing is often few drafts, readers still believe we must rewrite because they went to the same English classes we did. Duh.

So, out in public, you will hear me say simply that I am a three-draft writer. It's the truth. I write a first draft, I spell-check the manuscript as a second draft, and I fix the typos and small details my first reader finds as a third draft.

And after 100 plus novel sales and hundreds of short story sales, it seems to be working just fine.

For me, anyway.

Every Writer Is Different

If you are rewriting and not selling, try to stop rewriting for a year and just mail or publish your work. You might be stunned at what happens.

Just remember, the writing process has nothing to do with the finished work.

Never tell anyone you "cranked that off" or that it's a "first draft." Let them believe you worked like a ditch digger on the story, rewrote it 50 times, workshopped it a dozen times, and struggled over every word for seven years. Won't hurt your readers.

But getting rid of this myth for yourself sure might help your writing.

And make writing a ton more fun as well.

Sacred Cow #4

YOU MUST HAVE AN AGENT
TO SELL A BOOK

In the world that now has indie publishing as a viable path, that myth is just flat silly. But alas, the myth is very real and a foundation belief for a lot of writers who only want to go to traditional publishing.

To be clear, I like agents as people (for the most part) and have no desire to bring them harm. Most of them are decent people who love books. But there are a few out there who think nothing of taking a writer's money. However, most do try their best in a very tough new world.

The problem is that their place in the profession is going away quickly. I used to call agents the "wart on the butt of publishing" since they have no real job in the process of writing and publishing a book. But now that "wart" is about to come off completely.

But even with the place of agents in publishing fading fast, in the last 20 years the biggest myth that has blown up into a damaging myth is that you need an agent to sell a book. And the myth is holding on and killing many great dreams of writers.

Needing an agent to sell a book in 2013 is, of course, complete hogwash. But I have no doubt some of you reading this are already resisting this idea. You want someone to do the dirty work for you, to do the research, to just "take care of you" so you can just write. Yeah, that's going to happen. And in a way it will. They will "take care" of what little money you have and then kick you to the curb.

And even worse, the false myth that you need an agent to sell a book overseas or into translation or into movies has gotten worse since indie publishing started up, trapping many, many writers into thinking they needed to give a part of their work away to some scam agent. That part of this myth is also total hogwash.

All overseas contracts are in the language of the author and very, very simple and direct. Agents are the ones to make them complex and take a part of your money, if not all the money.

And for Hollywood, you need a Hollywood attorney if someone comes calling and is serious. The old joke used to be that the actress was so dumb, she slept with the writer. The joke is now that the actress was so dumb, she slept with the agent. Literary agents in Hollywood are long gone from a value position and lawyers have mostly taken their place, just as is slowly happening in book publishing.

Warning: The biggest place for scams with all agents and agencies is in overseas money. Most authors, even big names, never check money owed them with the overseas publisher as to how much they are supposed to be getting.

So to explain this "Agents Must Sell Books" myth clearly, I need to back up just a touch and run through some history to get to why this myth even exists and then move on into how to fight it.

Basic History

Book agents came over from theater and movies from 1900-1950. They were used by fiction writers to help with the contracts, to get the books into movie and early television (in New York) and overseas, and to go get the coffee. They were simply a lower-level employee used by writers to do some of the busy work.

It never occurred to most fiction writers to have an agent sell a book for them except in very unusual circumstances. Writers worked directly with the editors, and the idea that anyone needed to be in the middle of that was just thought of as silly.

But then, as the industry got bigger through the baby-boom years, fewer writers lived near New York and thus mailing manuscripts to editors started to become the norm. Editors and writers still worked together, and the agent did the deal, negotiating the contract, helping with contracts overseas and in Hollywood. But up until the early 1990s, book deals between editors and writers were often done across a dinner table with a handshake, with the agent left to handle the calls with the contract department later.

In fact, about twenty of my early novel deals were done over dinner up into the mid 1990s. I basically sold my first novel sitting in a bar, talking with an editor friend while waiting for a meeting with a person who would be my agent for the next seventeen years.

In those days editors had power to make deals as well. That is long gone now.

Also in those days, in the big New York publishers, there were rooms and rooms full of what is called "slush."

Now the term "slush pile" came from the early days of publishing. An editor usually sat at his desk and writers brought him work. But when the editor was gone and the office door closed, the writer still wanted to leave the manuscript, so they tossed it through the small window over the door. The top of the door is called a transom, so thus the term "over the transom" came into being.

When the editor returned to the office and pushed open the door, the manuscripts on the floor would be pushed into a pile which looked a lot like a pile of dirty New York snow. Thus the term "slush pile" came about.

In the early 1980s, publishers tried to slow down the growing wave of manuscripts coming at them by putting requirements on guidelines that no manuscript be sent unless it was solicited. A simple thing to ignore, and it stopped only the really stupid new writers.

Huge rooms of book manuscripts filled New York buildings and many, many assistant editors were hired to dig through the slush to find the gems among all the trash. And many, many major writers you read today came out of those slush piles.

Then in the 1990s, lots of things happened in publishing, not the least of which was a complete distribution system collapse. Publishers had to cut back, larger presses ate smaller ones, and at the same time New York real estate prices went up and up and up. Publishers could no longer afford the huge rooms full of slush, or the assistant editors to wade through it all.

At this point in time, agents were doing more and more for writers, and the top writers had very powerful agents, simply because the agents worked for the top writers. (Agents always used to get their power from their clients. They have no power on their own.)

Also, writers became more of an unknown to publishers, a vast sea of people with a computer and a stamp who thought they could write and should be rich even though they had never spent any time practicing their craft or even learning how to spell. Very few of these new writers ever thought of going to a writers' conference and actually meeting an editor, so editors became somewhat fearful of the nutballs out there.

And trust me, that fear was founded in reality. You ain't lived as an editor until you've had the FBI come and interview you about a writer making threats through the mail. Death threats because of rejections were fairly common, folks. I personally got three or four over the years.

Something had to be done to stop this massive wave coming at the money-worried publishers and overworked editors. So someone, somewhere, came up with the idea "Let the agents handle it."

So onto the guidelines of every publisher went the simple line. "No unagented manuscripts accepted." Even though most editors were still buying from writers without agents, or manuscripts from writers where the agent had not sent it in.

But every new writer believed that guideline, for some reason, without thought or reason or understanding of how publishing worked. Even editors at the time were surprised how well that one simple line worked to turn away the uninformed.

Thus, for the last fifteen years or more, agents have been getting buried with the vast amount of slush. Older agents went into hiding, knowing their job wasn't to read slush, and new scam agents popped up everywhere, taking advantage of this new guideline from publishers by milking the writer of their money and crushing their dreams.

It makes me very, very sad to think of the number of incredible books we have all missed because of this stupid one-sentence guideline.

Who Fights for the Writer?

Let's step back for a second and look at the relationship of agent/editor/writer/publisher in 2013.

First: A writer sells a publisher a manuscript and there is a contract between the publisher and writer. In simple business terms, the writer produces a product and goes into a partnership with a publisher to produce and distribute the product.

(In indie publishing, you are your own publisher, which makes it very simple.)

Second: The editor works for the publisher. Paid by the publisher, represents the publisher's needs.

Third: The agent used to work for the writer and fight for and represent the writer's needs. That's the belief, but sadly, it is no longer the truth.

Now, even though an agent gets paid by taking a percentage of the writer's work, the agents actually work for the publishers. Remember, the agents were the ones that accepted the outsourcing of the slush pile by the publishers. The agents can always find new writers these days. The agents can't find new publishers with (in their belief system) only the big five left.

This new relationship with publishers allows young agents to think they are the boss over writers. Of course, no long-term writer think this, and no respected, longer-term agent thinks it either (but there are only a few of those left anymore). Beginning writers and early professionals fall into this trap, and even go so far as to rewrite a book on demand of their agent.

If you are rewriting a book for an agent, just stop. For heaven's sake, indie publish the draft you mailed them first and get on with your life.

Agents can't buy books.

And keep this in mind very, very clearly if you are rewriting for an agent. If the agent could write, they would be, instead of taking 15% of what a writer makes for writing. Yet beginning writers and young professionals who don't understand how the business really works fall into this ugly rewriting trap all the time. This has gotten so bad, I try to not even listen when some poor sucker of a writer is telling me happily that they "got" an agent and are rewriting their book. Just turns my stomach.

So in this new world.

—Traditional publishers believe that writers are a dime-a-dozen and the publishers don't even want to bother with the writer's manuscripts.

—Editors work for the big corporation, thinking only bottom line.

—Agents work for the publishing houses, vetting slush and trying to keep their five editor-friends happy.

The writer is outnumbered and alone. Three parts of the old process now work for the big corporation. No one (but an attorney, if the writer is smart enough to hire one) is on the writer's side.

But we have a new secret weapon: **We don't need any of them anymore.**

And honestly, that's driving them nuts.

Who Can Be an Agent?

Can you have a business card printed up for you? Then you can be an agent. Actually, skip that, you don't even need a business card.

Anyone can be an agent. Anywhere.

There are no rules, no regulations, no training. The old joke is "What does it take to become a book agent? Stationery."

Yet new writers put their entire business, their entire dreams, their entire hopes for a future on someone who only needed stationery to get started.

See how silly this all is? And sad.

And what is even more scary is that writers give these total strangers all the money from their work and the paperwork that goes with that work. And then wonder why they get ripped off.

Here is how it really works when put in real world terms.

You go to a hotel and meet a total stranger. They agree to take months of your work and sell it, then you trust this total stranger after they have sold your work with getting you all the money from your work and all the paperwork for that money. You don't know the person.

And only in publishing do otherwise sane and smart business people think this sort of thing makes sense.

Literary agents are not regulated at all. (We all have watched in the financial world and how well unregulated people do with money.) Yet new writers, without research, hire an agent and give them control over all their income.

If you don't think the Madoff types also live in the agent world, you are sadly kidding yourself. And they make a fortune, mostly off of big name writers who can't be bothered to keep track of their own money. Not kidding.

"My Agent Is Good" Myth

Every professional writer I know who has an agent (and has yet to discover the agent is taking their money or stopping deals or not sending in books) thinks their agent is the exception. It's the "I believe you, Dean, but it doesn't apply to my agent" syndrome. The "My Agent is Good" myth is deeper than any of these myths combined. Only when a writer gets screwed or their money taken or they are dumped by their "perfect agent" for asking for something to be done, does the writer finally step back and understand. Sometimes. But sometimes the writer just runs to another agent and starts again. The myth is that deep

If you think your agent works for anyone but themselves and the publishers in 2014, you are really, really deluding yourself.

But, of course, your agent is the exception... right?

And keep this question firmly in mind...

How does my agent pay to live in New York, have an office, have employees, on 15% of book advances that have declined by factors of ten over the last few years?

Answer: **They can't and won't for long.**

So when it comes down to paying their mortgage and buying food vs. sending you the money a publisher sent to them on your latest royalty (remember they have all the paperwork), they will pay their own mortgage and buy the food with your money. They will think you won't notice it being late for a month or so. And then when you don't notice at all that you didn't get that royalty statement from Germany (or your US publisher because you are writing and can't be bothered,) they just "forget" to get around to sending the money to you.

So unless you are talking with every one of your publishers, and know exactly when every penny is coming to you and how much, your "Perfect" agent will stay in business on your back. Sorry. Just reality.

And big agencies are the worst at this, folks. Far worse, because they have accounting departments and the agents in big agencies usually get a base salary.

You get your money stolen, you have no one to blame but yourself. You gave a perfect stranger all the control of your work, your money, and the paperwork with that money. You deserve what you get or don't get, I'm afraid.

Solution?

We live in a wonderful new publishing world where agents are just flat useless.

Their place in the industry is fading away and they know it, which is why so many of them have set up publishing arms to "help" their clients out of even more of their rights and money. That's right, every major agency now has a "publishing arm" to scam their clients by taking fifteen percent for work the writer could easily do themselves and faster and better.

So back to the point of this myth. How do you sell a book to a traditional publishing house without an agent?

Two ways here in 2014, and not one of them involve an agent.

First, indie publish your book and then keep writing. Sure, there is a slight learning curve of covers and blurbs and such, but if your books get traction, traditional publishers will come calling and you will be able to actually negotiate a contract with some clout because they want your book. And you will know what your book is worth.

This happens every day now.

But a warning. If your book is making $3,000 per month for you in indie publishing, you might not want to sell it or any book for a $10,000 advance for the life of the contract. (grin)

Second method, mail the book directly to an editor. This has sort of come around to where it was when I started off. You must meet editors and be a nice business person and talk with them directly.

You need to go out and meet some editors at writers' conferences and conventions. So while all your idiot friends are crowding around the agents, make an appointment with an editor and pitch your book. Know ahead of time what the editor publishes and be nice. Let me stress the **be nice and professional** part.

If the editor gives you a card and asks you to send the book, you are in the editor's door and on their desk without an agent. You have become one of their writers.

Oh, wait, one more way...

Third: DO BOTH AT THE SAME TIME. Why wait around with your book when indie publishing won't hurt it in anyone's eyes in New York?

Just a thought.

One final point on this:

New writers today are *still* flooding agents with manuscripts and great books and writers are being lost in this ugliness. This myth will only go away over time, more than likely the next twenty years or so, as writers take back control and start realizing there are more ways to get into traditional publishing than by giving away part of their work.

I've sold over a hundred novels to traditional publishers and I sure can't see myself going back until traditional publishers stop some of their contractual practices, but that's another article. But if I did go back, I sure wouldn't use an agent.

Traditional publishing is in a period of major transition. It will survive, but not in a form we would recognize now, or with many of the names that are now in business.

Agents will not survive. At least the non-scam ones.

Sacred Cow #5

BOOKS ARE EVENTS
(Or put as clearly as I can...)

ALL BOOKS NEED TO BE EVENTS,
NEED TO BE SOMETHING SPECIAL

Hogwash, of course. All books must be written as well as the author can write the book, but just because the author spent blood and sweat on the book, or the author wrote it in twenty days, doesn't make the book either special or not special. And it certainly doesn't make it an event.

Hard and fast rule about writing:

THE PROCESS AND EXPERIENCE OF THE AUTHOR IN THE WRITING OF THE BOOK HAS NOTHING AT ALL TO DO WITH THE FINAL QUALITY OF THE BOOK.

If you put that on your wall, you will always have a defense against many of the things I'm going to talk about in this chapter.

When is a book an **actual** event? Let me answer that question before I move on to other areas of this topic, the deadly areas and the areas that are hurting many writers and indie publishers.

1) A book is an actual event when an author finishes his or her first novel.

Now, that's something special and should be celebrated with friends and family with a good dinner, maybe cards, flowers, something special like a cake. Finishing a first novel puts the writer in a very small minority of writers. Most writers talk about writing, but never find the time to write, let alone to do what it takes to write an entire novel, working for weeks or months to do it. Finishing a first novel is a small event. Celebrate, then put the novel in the mail and get started on the next one.

Kevin J. Anderson sent me a great card after I finished my first novel. On the face of the card are four pictures of a very small mouse pushing a huge elephant up a steep hill. When you open the card, it shows the mouse, sweating, with the elephant at the top of the hill, and at the base of the hill is a herd of elephants just waiting. The caption says, "Great work! Now, do it again."

Spot on the money.

2) Publishing a first novel is an actual event. In the old world of traditional publishing it most likely wasn't your first novel written, but it will always be considered your first novel from that publication forward. My first novel is *Laying the Music to Rest,* which was the third book I wrote. That first publication should be celebrated, and I remember I did. It is very special, and that specialness needs to be acknowledged by both the author and everyone around them. That is an actual event. Enjoy it!

So Why Is Making a Book an Event So Bad?

About a hundred different reasons, so let me start slowly into the thinking that kills author after author on this myth. And frighteningly enough, this is the myth that I fight the most. This myth has cost me years of my writing career.

Years. And I am not kidding.

And I am watching it kill indie writer after indie writer already in this new world.

In the Beginning...

None of us start out as novelists. No one. Sorry, doesn't happen.

We all learn to write in school, from teachers, from hundreds of people along the way. And often writers start by writing poems, short stories, things like that, even when starting into fiction decades after they learned to write their first sentence. Novels are those big, complex things in a beginning writer's mind that need to have a ton of time spent on them to do correctly. (See the myth about writing fast.)

And all believe we must write the book from word one to the last word because that's how readers read them. And that must take time and effort and be really hard because it seems complex. And almost magical.

Why do we all have this belief? Because before starting to write novels, we all read novels, and they seemed complex, they seemed long, they seemed just flat hard to do. We built them up to be something really special before we even wrote word one of a novel.

So here comes something like the November novel challenge that happens every year. Thousands and thousands of people manage to write at least 50,000 words in a month or less. Many of them found it easy, many of them had a blast doing it.

But alas, to most of them the book they produced can't be any good **because** it was fun to do, it was easy to do, and gasp, it was written quickly.

The thinking is that novels have to be hard and complex and thus because it was fun and easy and quick, it can't be good. In other words... **A novel must be an EVENT in the writing process**.

Total hogwash, of course. Back to the only solid rule in writing.

THE PROCESS AND EXPERIENCE OF THE AUTHOR IN THE WRITING OF THE BOOK HAS NOTHING AT ALL TO DO WITH THE FINAL QUALITY OF THE BOOK.

Book as Event thinking puts thousands and thousands of great books into drawers every December 1st because the author had too much fun writing it.

Not kidding.

Writers don't mail books or indie publish the book because they enjoyed writing it.

This myth is that stupid. And that deadly.

It Must Be Perfect.

Book as Event really hits right here, kicking in the myth that everything must be rewritten to death before it can be good. A book must be worked over and over and over to make it "perfect." Hogwash, simple hogwash.

So how do you write a novel? Simply do the best you can every day during the writing, finish the book, fix the mistakes a trusted first reader finds, and mail the thing or publish the thing and start the next book.

There is no such thing as a perfect book and the more you work to make a book perfect, the more you turn it into a polished stone with no character or voice. Leave your book rough, leave your voice alone, mail the book to an editor or indie publish the book and do another.

Repeat after me....**There is no perfect book.**

Never has been, never will be. *And you certainly won't write the first one.* Sorry.

Senator Ted Kennedy had a great quote that my wife has on her wall in her office. "Never let perfect be the enemy of the good."

But...but...but...

Yeah, I can hear you all starting into that thinking. So let me start with a few of the doubts I can hear creeping into this.

Doubt #1. "If I don't write a perfect book, it will be rejected in this tough market. Or readers won't buy it even if I discount it to 99 cents."

Wrong. Books are bought for story. Sure, keep the spelling mistakes and typing mistakes down to a minimum by having some trusted first readers and a good proofreader, but your story won't be rejected for a few bad sentences if the story is kick-ass. Novels are simply stories, nothing more. Write a good story, get it out for readers to find, write another.

Doubt #2 "But I want my story to be perfect, my characters big, my plot flawless."

To do that, you have to trust your subconscious, and *that part of your brain **only** functions in fast, first-draft mode.*

You come at your book from critical brain, and you'll end up writing like your first-grade teacher, without voice or anything original left in the book.

There are many more doubts, many more. I know, I've had them, and fell for some of them along the way. But for the moment, back to the bigger topic.

This Is Too Hard.

If you feel that way in a book, you are trapped in a myth somewhere, more than likely **Book as Event**.

When did writing a story become hard? It's not, no matter what authors want to tell you at conventions and writers' conferences and on their blogs. And I have done a chapter on this as well coming up.

The truth: Writing a story is fun.

And those of us lucky enough to do it for a living have the best job in the world, period. I sit alone in a room and make stuff up and people pay me large sums of money to do that. And readers buy my stories and sometimes even write me fan letters. What is so hard about that?

But when it starts feeling hard, when the voices start creeping in that the story sucks while you are writing, that the plot doesn't work, that even your first-grade teacher will hate you when they see the crap you are writing, then guess what? You are trapped in **Book as Event** myth.

A book is not an event. It is just a long story. Nothing more. And nothing less.

Tell the story, move on to another one. And have fun. You could be digging a ditch in the rain.

It Must Be Art.

Oh, heavens, if that is your thinking, you are lost. Way, way deep in **Book as Event**.

If you think every book you write must be art, stop writing now, which more than likely you already have. There is no such thing as the "Great American Novel" anymore, and I sort of doubt there ever was, actually. I have a hunch that was a myth made up way back.

The truth is that in traditional publishing every month thousands of publishers and imprints must fill a monthly list. Those lists must be filled to keep the machine of publishing going. And now, with electronic publishing, the slots needed for novels is increasing even faster.

No book will climb above that crowd, at least not as art. Your book may climb above it as a bestseller, but if you are thinking you are writing art, I'm sure you look down your nose at bestsellers. Go study the history of the books that are considered art today and you might have a hope of getting over that, since most of the books studied as art today were the bestsellers of their time.

Art needs audience.

If you are selling your book that took six years to write to 200 people, you are not writing art. Sorry.

(Oh, that's going to make some people angry. Sigh...)

To Sell More Copies, My Book Must Be Bigger.

I have to admit, I fell for this one as well for a few years, as did most of publishing because of the collapse of the distribution system in the mid 1990s. I even taught a class here on the coast in how to write a "Big Book." Worst class I ever taught, and most destructive to writers. Sorry, those of you who took it.

A story just is what it needs to be.

Some stories are small, some fit in niches, some sprawl large and wide. Whatever you want to write, let your story be what it wants to be. Then when you are finished, figure out how to market it and get it to readers. Then get started on the next book.

I Have to Promote My New Book...

This comes from **Book as Event** myth as well.

I have a chapter later in this book on promotion. Promotion thinking has come solidly into indie publishing because no one really knows what works. So writer after writer on blog after blog talk about how they promoted their new book. That just makes me shudder, to be honest.

Not a one of these "indie promotion specialists" trust their own book to be good enough to attract readers. They all assume that because they did promotion their book sold. Wow, what little understanding of readers these people have.

Books don't sell because you promoted it. Books sell because they are good stories readers want to read. Nothing more.

I am a believer that more writing promotes writing better than anything artificial an author can do. Just because you finished a novel doesn't mean you have to spend six months promoting it. Why not spend those same six months writing the next one or two novels?

Yet this **Book as Event** thinking is causing writer after writer to stop writing and promote their last book. What a waste of time.

And if you really want to know how to promote a book that won't kill your writing and help you understand what is a waste of time or not, Kris and I have put together an online promotions workshop. If you are having trouble clearing this myth, you might want to take that workshop.

But remember one thing about promotion to an extreme: It's like walking through life backwards, always looking back and paying attention to what you have done in the past, not what you are going to do in the future.

Face forward.

Remember, writers are people who write. Authors are people who have written (and are now promoting).

Be a writer.

Eating the Elephant.

That's what Kris and I call the problem writers have when they can't seem to start something. If you were standing beside a well-cooked elephant and your task was to eat every bite of the huge thing, you would say you couldn't do it. But, actually, you could. One bite at a time, over a period of time.

Novels are the same thing. They are mostly impossible to hold completely in your mind, so when starting it looks like a huge task (book as event again) and thus it's just easier to not start, easier to keep outlining and plotting and researching and doing all those things that are not writing.

The key is to just start, write so much per day, stop when you find the ending, and then mail it or indie publish it. (Yup, sort of like many of you do in the November challenge.)

This problem stops all of us at times. Even someone like me who has sold over 100 novels to traditional publishers, and written more than that number. I have a sign over my computer that says simply "Trust the Process" and it's right beside another sign. "Write Scenes."

Scenes I can hold in my head. Write a scene, then write the next scene, and trust the process as the days and weeks go by.

Summary

This topic is so huge, and this problem so big, that I'm sure I'm missing areas of it. I will try to cover those areas in other chapters along the way.

But in short, the myth of **Book as Event** is the underlying problem most writers face all the time.

It's easy to start building up a book into something more than it really is, especially when people ask "How's your book coming?" That question sort of underlines that the book is an event, and that it is the only book you have in you.

I once had a guy come up to me and say, "I hear you have a book coming out?" That year I had eleven novels coming out, just about one every month. So I said, "Sure do."

Being a nice guy, he said, "I'm looking forward to reading it. What's the title?"

I said, "Which one?"

He looked puzzled, like it didn't make sense that I had more than one book coming out. To him, and to most folks, writing and publishing a book are huge events, so how could it be possible to have more than one?

When I tried to help him and said, "I have five books in the next five months coming out," he looked horrified.

Right now, quickly check in with yourself.

—Do you feel horrified by the idea that I published eleven novels in twelve months one year?

—Do you think that because I did that, those books must automatically be bad?

If those thoughts passed through your mind, then you have an issue with the myth of **Book as Event**.

And that myth will stop you in one way or another, at one point or another.

So, if you just finished a book and are making up excuses to not mail it to editors or not get it out indie published because you had too much fun writing it, because it came too fast or too easy, or it needs a massive rewrite, you really have issues with **Book as Event** thinking.

Just because a book is fun to write, just because you wrote it fast, just because you don't think it's any good, doesn't mean it's a bad book.

In fact, it usually means it's a pretty darned good book.

Have fun getting it published.

And then get writing on the next one.

Sacred Cow #6

SELLING A NOVEL TO TRADITIONAL PUBLISHING WILL GUARANTEE THE NOVEL IS QUALITY

(Or Conversely)

NOT SELLING A NOVEL TO TRADITIONAL PUBLISHING WILL MEAN THE NOVEL IS NOT QUALITY

This myth is so flat wrong in so many ways, I'm not sure where to begin. But wow do you hear this everywhere.

In fact, I have seen it even with successful indie-published writers. I have watched in horror as indie writers (making great money) have fallen for this myth by suddenly turning and selling to traditional publishers, even though they would make more money and get to more readers just by continuing on what they were doing.

So let me outline how I will attack this myth before giving some history, as I always do.

Here are the three main areas of thinking this myth falls into.

1) Because a book is bought by a large traditional publisher, the book is quality.

2) Because a book is not bought by a large traditional publisher, the book is not good enough to be published.

3) I am a new writer. How do I determine if my book is of "good enough" quality to be published?

Some History

Am I immune to this thinking of worrying about quality? Nope.

I was raised to read and was in school just as most of us were. In school, all books were things that had knowledge, were special, or (in the case of fiction I believed) were written by "gods" who took me to wonderful new places, strange planets, and fantastic space-ships. In fact, it never really dawned on me that real people wrote books until I owned a bookstore and started seeing so many thousands and thousands of books pour through. Some I liked, some I didn't, and some I wondered why anyone would even publish it.

We all were raised to think that something in a book is "important." And then (as we got older) we developed reading tastes. We discovered what kind of writing we liked, what our favorite genre was, and who our favorite writers were.

And we all bought books exactly the same as editors buy books. That's right, exactly the same.

We walk into a bookstore, pick up a book that looks inter-esting, read the back cover, then maybe read the first few pages and then (horrors) actually flip to the back to see how the book ended before we plunked down our money. We still do that now with electronic books by glancing at the blurb and cover, then reading the sample before buying. Same as in a bookstore.

In large traditional publishing, an editor gets a novel manuscript that looks interesting, reads the first few pages, flips to the proposal to see what the book is about, then reads to the end to see how the book ends. And then if the editor likes the book, she fights for it through the system of sales and art departments and so on. But the key is she has to like the book, just as you have to like a book before you spend money on it.

We are all editors editing for our own personal reading lists.

You may personally think Clive Cussler or Danielle Steele or Nora Roberts are bad writers, but millions of other independent editors don't agree with you.

You buy for what you think is quality writing and storytelling and what you enjoy reading. And what you think will differ from what I think and what millions of others will think. And what most traditional publishing editors will think as well.

Thankfully, that's the way it works. Always has.

The Limitations of Traditional Fiction Editors

Editors working for large traditional publishers are just people too. Heck, I've edited at times, remember.

Editors have huge restrictions on them that have nothing to do with the quality of a story. For example, the best story I ever got in the ten years editing for *Star Trek* was by a wonderful mystery writer named Julie Hyzy. It was a story that I couldn't buy. All these years later that story is as clear to me as the day it knocked me out of my chair when I read it. But because no traditional publisher could buy that story, does that mean it was low quality?

Of course not. Julie was then, and still is, one of the best writers I know.

I couldn't buy it for reasons that had nothing to do with quality. Nothing at all. I couldn't buy the story because it didn't fit into the very narrow restrictions I had on what I could buy as an editor.

Every editor is exactly the same way, and these days, the restrictions are even narrower because of sales departments and publishers not wanting to take a chance on anything different or unusual. At this point, if you don't have something that is almost guaranteed to make money, publishers won't look. They are that scared.

So let me detail out the hurdles you have to jump through to get an editor to buy your book.

— *You must mail it to an editor, or get it through an agent to an editor who might buy it. (This step stops most writers these days.)*

— *The editor must love the book, meaning it must fit into the editor's taste area.*

— *The editor must think the book will fit in what the company publishes and what she can buy for her list.*

— *The editor must get someone in sales to think the book will sell.*

— *The editor must often get another editor to like the book*

— *The editor must get the publisher to sign off on the book in a corporate meeting.*

Wow, are there a lot of steps between a writer finishing a book and an editor making an offer. And don't forget that process often takes years.

And millions and millions of quality books (books that would find their share of readers if all things were equal) are eliminated by this process. (Luckily, with indie publishing, things are quickly becoming equal.)

So let me deal with the three major areas this myth hits that I outlined back at the beginning.

1) Because a novel is bought by a large traditional publisher, the book is quality.

This part of this myth is very, very deep inside all of us. We all think that because a large traditional publisher spent money and time to publish a book, it is automatically quality. I have heard this lately called "the stamp of approval" and "validation" by different writers.

The truth is that for the one house, the one editor, the book was quality. But I can't begin to point out the millions of examples of novels published for one reason or another by a traditional publisher that just sucked, were poorly written, and worse yet, poorly proofed and typeset and laid out.

In fact, I don't know if many of you have noticed, but at this point in time, the traditionally published books are much worse in format and proofing than what indie publishers are doing. Much, much worse.

Thinking of all traditional fiction publishers as one large great judge of books is just flat wrong.

A few people, sometimes less than two or three, are in charge of getting a traditionally published novel out to readers. Sure, there are others along the way, but only the editor, a sales person, and a publisher are the judges of quality of the book. And often one or two of them are missing in the equation.

An ugly secret: Very, very often the editor is the only person in a publishing company who has actually read the entire book.

Sorry, but true. The others have just read samples or pitches for the book the editor put together. Not kidding.

Another ugly secret... I know of a number of books that never got read at all by anyone in the publishing house, just sent in and published. (Yup, traditional publishers are great judges of work, especially when no one reads the book.)

When I learned this fact early on in my editing life, I actually was depressed. I had always believed that if a big traditional publisher put out a story, it was like the book was sent from some publishing god to the readers with some special secret stamp of approval.

To be honest, I hated the fact that I could pick a story as an editor and give that story some sort of special magical powers of sudden quality. And that story would get published and I would have been the only person to read it.

In the final result, all I was giving the story or book was very much like a reviewer gives a novel. I was saying I liked it. Nothing more.

Let me repeat that: **NOTHING MORE.**

Editors are humans who have likes and dislikes. Sure, we all try to pick the best stories, but they are always the stories we think are the best in our opinion.

And trust me, we can all be wrong. Very, very wrong.

And often are.

2) Because a book is not bought by a large traditional publisher, the book is not good enough to be published.

With the state of traditional publishing at the moment, with the slush out-sourced, with editors tied by sales force demands, with companies barely holding on and trying to make changes to electronic sales, very few high-quality books with top stories are getting through. And it is often not the highest-quality story or novel that gets through, but instead it's the story that has the most marketability according to *the opinion of* a sales person. Who maybe only read a one-page summary of the book.

Thinking that a story isn't quality if it doesn't sell to a traditional publisher is just flat silly.

Let me give you a personal example: I have exactly 250 rejections for different stories from five different editors of *Asimov's Science Fiction Magazine*. That's right, from the very beginning of the magazine I was pounding on that door and not once did I sell a story to them. Not once.

Should I think that all my stories are not quality because I can't sell to that magazine and those five different editors over three decades? Nope. They just didn't fit because my short stories tend to be slightly off of center, to put it mildly. I have later sold almost all of those stories. But thankfully I never believed this part of this myth, or I wouldn't have kept the stories out there in the mail and eventually sold them.

3) I am a new writer. How do I determine if my book is of "good enough" quality to be published?

This is the difficult subject to talk about because all new writers must go through a learning curve to get craft up to certain "levels" that will allow readers to follow your story and stay involved with your story.

And trust me, for an experienced editor, it is easy to see at a glance a new writer who hasn't written enough words and studied enough to get craft up to a level anyone but family is going to want to read. What tips us off? Oh, easy things like no setting, no voice, characters you can't tell apart, walking from one part of the story to the other. All stuff that would make a reader put the book down and not buy it.

Notice I did not say sentence-by-sentence writing... At this point in history most everyone can write a decent sentence. Quality writing does not mean quality typing. **It means quality storytelling.**

The old method was to just write and submit and when your storytelling craft started climbing some of your stories started breaking through the editorial roadblocks and got to readers. That system was pretty clear for most, but wow did it fail writers with very unusual voices or stories that did not fit into certain genres. Those writers never did get through the system for the most part. Like I haven't got through the system yet at *Asimov's*.

But now we have a new world in which writers can publish their own stuff, and in a past blog, I talked about writers just publishing their own book and then mailing the trade paper book to traditional publishers as part of the submission package. I can't begin to tell you how many letters I got asking the question "How do I know if my book is good enough to be published?"

Back to #1 category above, writers think that just because a book is published, it has to be quality. So if the new writer publishes their own book in trade paper, it has to be quality before they dare do that. Right?

Nope. Just publish the thing and move on.

But how do they know if it is quality?

And the circular logic goes around and around and around.

HOW DOES ANY WRITER OF ANY LEVEL KNOW THAT A STORY IS QUALITY?

Short answer: They don't. We don't.

Long answer: They don't and never will, even if the story is published by a traditional publisher.

Being published by a traditional publisher means a book is liked by a few people. Put the book up on your own on Amazon and B&N and Smashwords and iBooks and Sony and Kobo and others and see how many people buy it.

In this new world, it is time to start trusting readers.

Why not do a POD version and use it as part of a submission package to a traditional publisher if that is still your goal?

Why not?

The answer to all this again comes down to writers and their belief systems. At this moment in history, most writers and all newer writers have no backbone.

Writers (as a class) do not believe that their work is their art. And they are not willing to defend it and keep learning from their mistakes and keep working to make their art better.

But, of course, my advice about "grow a backbone" has been ignored for years now in many of these chapters, so let me see if I can give a few more concrete guidelines. But realize, these are just my opinions and I am only one person.

How Do I Know if My Book Is "Good Enough" to Be Published?
(Dean's Opinion of What to Do)

1) How many words have you written in fiction since you started trying to write? Mystery Grand Master John D. Mc-Donald used to say that all writers starting out had a million words of crap in them. I started selling stories just short of the million word mark and have sold some of my stories that I wrote between half-million and that first million. However, because of a house fire, I can't look back on any of the words before that.

But if you have a bunch of stories done, maybe a novel, and have been working at writing for a time, I think you are more than safe to let readers be the judge.

2) Realize that you may have paid your storytelling dues in other areas besides fiction. Say if you have written a couple dozen plays and had a couple produced, your storytelling skills are probably pretty good. If you've been a reporter or worked nonfiction. Things like that. Lots of other areas transfer over into fiction writing. In that case you might be writing quality fiction right from the first hundred thousand words.

3) How much are you studying writing to become a better storyteller? If you only have three how-to-write books on your shelf and have never even listened to a professional writer speak at a conference, you may be way ahead of yourself in thinking of publishing.

In other words, in short, what I am talking about is a learning period, and the learning must go hand-in-hand with the typing.

It's called "practice" in any other art. In writing you need to practice as well.

But you want my honest opinion?

Put the story up and let the readers decide. Right from the first story.

Writers are always the worst judges of their own work.

And readers who pay money always trump any other source of feedback.

So grow a backbone and trust your work and get it out there, either to a traditional publisher or electronically and POD published.

So What Is the Downside of Self-Publishing Too Early?

Nothing.

No one buys your book, it sinks like a stone because it is a poor story, and eventually (in a couple of years), as you keep learning, you pull it down and put it out of print.

Here is the problem that beginning writers have on this issue: *Beginning writers are staring at their own navels.*

What I mean by that is new beginning writers are so worried about sentences and pretty words and nifty grammar and pleasing their workshop that they forget they are storytellers.

They are not working to become entertainers, but instead they just work on good sentences. Beginning writers just forget about readers and how readers are the real judges.

There are no repercussions for publishing a book in electronic or POD format and it not selling.

Well, maybe your oversized ego gets bumped some because you believed that you could be as good as Stephen King with your first novel and didn't have to do the decades of work and learning that King did. Get over it and get learning and practicing.

And what is even more frightening... If you publish a book that doesn't work, no one will come to your house and shoot you. No one will blackball you from all of publishing. No one will even notice, which is even worse than the first two. At least on the first two someone noticed your book.

You think people will notice; you think a bad book will ruin your career. Nope. You have no career to ruin as a new writer.

So what happens...

You put up your own new book and it sucks. No one will buy it, and no one will notice and it will sink without a trace.

And you can promote it to your heart's content, sell it for 99 cents because Locke or someone else without a real belief in their own work did that, and still no one will buy it because they will look at the sample and think, "Nope this book isn't for me." And those readers will not buy it and they will not remember your name.

But if they like it.... Well, that's another story.

My Advice to Beginning Writers

1) Never stop writing and learning. Never think you know it all after a few sales. Never believe you are good enough. Learning in this business never, ever ends.

2) Keep your work for sale somewhere, either on editor's desks in New York or self-published or both. You are like an artist with your work hanging in an art gallery or a musician working a small bar. You are practicing and earning from your skill as it grows. It might not be much at first, but if you keep learning and practicing, the sales and the money will come with time.

3) Don't be in a hurry. This is an international business. You can't get there overnight. Put your work out for sale one way or another and then focus on the next book. Never look back. Leave the book up and alone. Have a five- and ten-year plan.

4) Grow a backbone. Believe in your own art without cutting off the learning. No writing is perfect and maybe a few people out there will think it works just fine and enjoy it. No book is perfect.

5) Never do anything that gets in the way of the writing. Stay away from stupid, time-wasting self-promotion beyond your own website and tiny bit of social media, and just write the next story and the next book. In other words, be a writer, a person who writes. And rewriting is not writing.

6) And most of all, have fun. If you are not having fun while at the same time being scared to death, get off this roller coaster. The ride only gets more extreme and more fun the farther you go along the track.

Trust me, folks, you don't want to put all your hopes and fears and beliefs that a work is quality on the judgment of an editor somewhere.

Sacred Cow #7

TO SELL EITHER TO EDITORS OR READERS, YOU MUST WRITE WHAT IS HOT

This myth stops thousands and thousands of book sales and destroys careers.

And it's just stupid, even though the myth seems to have a logical base in publishing.

This myth spouts like a bad cold out of the mouths of top professionals all the time in one form or another, and usually with the best of intentions. And it has for as long as I have been in this business.

And beginning indie writers repeat this over and over like it's a bad chant from a long lost tribe of magic aliens.

But lately, with the advent of the slush-reading lower-level agents and with the indie publishing revolution, this myth has taken on very, very deadly consequences for many writers.

Why? **Because they believe it.**

Hook, line, and sinker.

So as I do in these chapters, let me take a look at the origin of this myth first.

It Came From the Editors

Actually, the origin is simple. It came about back in the dark old days of traditional-only publishing because editors and agents and publishers want to make an easy sale.

Yes, editors sell books as well. They sell a book they love to their publisher, they sell the book to a sales force, and they ultimately are responsible for selling a book to readers. Books that are different, that don't fit in **what has been done before**, are very, very difficult sales for editors and publishers and always have been.

And it has been proven that if a reader likes a certain type of book, they will look for that type of book.

Now remember, publishers need so many books per month in this churn of book lists, so they have to find books to buy, and when they can find an easy-sell book, it makes their job easier.

And it's human nature to want to have your job be easier.

Of course, easy-sell books are usually pretty flat. (Not always, but usually.) They are often following a trend. The books tend to do little if anything new, which is why they are easy sells. And never remembered.

Another book bought by a more gutsy editor has already paved the way. Easy-sell books are also easy to promote. "If you liked 'X Book' you're going to love 'X Book Almost-The-Same.'"

Easy sell. Editors and publishers and corporate sales forces love them.

Now understand, I wrote a ton of easy-sell books. Media books such as Star Trek have a pretty set audience a publisher can depend on. So when Pocket Books came to me to write some Star

Trek novels, they knew exactly what the book would sell and so did I. Easy, no thought on the publisher's part.

What was a hard-sell book was *Star Trek: Strange New Worlds*. It took John Ordover years of fighting to get that series going and the fact that Pocket Books kept it going for ten years was not because of sales, but reasons of relationships with readers and Paramount.

Interestingly enough, over the history of publishing, the really monster books, the ones that people talk about and remember for decades, were not easy-sell books. Often they would have fifty or more rejections before finding an editor willing to work for the book and a publisher took a chance. Then (when the book became a hit) it was called new and fresh and readers loved it.

And hard-sell books are flat impossible to get through agents in this new world. Agents give up submitting books after four or five rejections and often drop clients who force them to submit books that are not easy-sell books. (Remember, these days agents work for publishers, not writers.)

And even worse, writers allow agents to have them rewrite their work to make it more of an easy-sell, thus killing any original work in the book.

And when somehow that fresh idea, fresh book does get through an editor and gets published, (in this new world, more than likely indie published first), it will spawn (like a bad horror movie) thousands of "easy sell" books.

But no one has made much of a long career writing only easy-sell books, because the target just keeps moving. One day one topic is hot, the next day the next topic is hot.

As a writer, if you try to chase that "hot-topic easy-sell" thinking, you might sell a few books, but you are lost in short order.

But then come editors and agents sitting on panels at writers' conferences telling new writers what they are looking for, what's selling, what isn't selling. In all honest truth, as an editor, I didn't know what I wanted to buy until I read it.

And as an editor for *Star Trek: Strange New Worlds* for ten years, I constantly told writers I hated the character "Q" from Next Generation. But I always ended up buying a "Q" story because some writer wrote one so well, with such a fun twist, that I couldn't not buy it.

Attempting to write what is hot isn't a new trend. It has been around since the beginning of this business. And the myth that you need to write what is hot, what is selling is as deadly today as it was fifty years ago. Honest, even in the new world of indie publishing, this myth will just kill your career and the fun in your writing fairly quickly.

So Why Is This Myth So Deadly?

The answer to that question is back in the writer's office. Each writer is different. Every chapter in this book I have been pounding that simple fact home.

Every writer is different.

Let me say that one more time:

Every Writer is Different!

And what makes your books interesting to readers is YOU.

I have also warned about taking the YOU out of your work over and over in these chapters as well. You can't see or hear your voice because to you it sounds dull because you hear it all the time. So when you rewrite something to death, you are taking the "you" out of your work.

And your ideas might seem dull because guess why? **They are yours!** Duh. They are as unique as you are, as how you write the ideas down.

But then you go trying to imitate some other writer, try to write what is "hot" because some editor or agent or writers' board told you that is what is selling. So what do you do? You take the YOU out of your work and it becomes mundane and just like everything else and won't sell.

Or if it does sell, it vanishes in the flood of sameness.

A SIMPLE RULE: In fiction, sameness and dullness do not sell.

Yet when a new writer hears an editor or agent or a bunch of writers on a writing board tell them what they "should" write to sell more, the young writer goes home and attempts to imitate the book everyone said they are looking for. They create nothing unique, nothing new, nothing of themselves. They write the same boring old crap that has already been done to death.

And this gets even worse in the circle-jerk thinking of places like online indie boards. You see talk about writing what is selling the most at the moment. That is the quickest way to writer death I have ever seen. It quickly forces a writer to get frustrated because "It was supposed to sell and make me millions, just like George R.R. Martin, but I only sold three copies last month."

So How Do You Solve This Problem?

Simple: Kick all the editor and agent and online board voices out of your writing office and write what makes you passionate or angry or excited.

Or as Stephen King has said, "Write what scares hell out of you."

Some basic guidelines on how to do this:

1) Never talk about your story with anyone ahead of time.

Their ideas, unless you are very experienced, will twist your original story into partially their story.

2) For heaven's sake, never, ever let anyone read a work-in-progress.

Totally stupid on so many levels I can't even begin to address. If you want to collaborate, make sure you have a collaboration agreement, otherwise, keep your work to yourself until finished.

And wow does this apply to workshops. Never show a work-in-progress. Ever. Trust yourself for heaven's sake and learn how to be an artist.

3) Never think of markets or selling when writing.

Enjoy the process of writing and creating a story. When the story is finished, then have someone read it and tell you what you wrote and then market it.

I get this question more than any other question. Should I write this to sell? Should I do this to have a career? And so on and so on. Folks, write what you want to write. Every writer is different, and if you celebrate that difference, you will eventually find an audience.

4) Follow Heinlein's Rules, especially #3 about never rewriting.

In other words, fix mistakes and then mail it and trust your own voice, your own work. Never rewrite to anyone's suggestions, especially a workshop.

And never use the word "polish" in front of me. When you take a unique piece of work and polish it, you make it look like all the others. And that's dull.

5) When an editor says they are looking for a certain type of book, ignore it.

They are just trying to be helpful to all the new writers looking for shortcuts to getting published. There are no shortcuts.

When agents say what they think will sell to editors, just laugh. I mean laugh really, really, really hard. They have less of a clue what will sell than anyone in the business, bar none. If agents really knew, they would write it themselves and keep all the millions.

I had an eye-opening moment one year when I asked a major agent what was the last book the agent read for pleasure. The agent couldn't remember because it had been years. The agent only had time to read what his/her clients were sending. Yet I heard this same person sit on a panel in front of a large group of beginning writers and go on about what the trends in reading were and what was selling in publishing. And yet they hadn't read a single book by anyone but their own clients. Yeah, trust that person's opinion to really make a career. Head-shaking it is so stupid.

6) Get passionate and protective of what you write.

It's your voice, your work, for heaven's sake, **grow a backbone and stand up for it.**

Sure, in the first million words you are going to need all sorts of help with craft and storytelling issues. Go learn that and take it in and study and practice and get feedback. **And never stop learning.** Make learning a regular part of your writing life.

But don't rewrite anything beyond fixing typos and mistakes. When you write a story or novel, trust yourself, trust your own art, and get it out to readers in one way or another.

Protect it from all who want you to write what they think you **should** have written.

Summary

So, in short, I am telling you flatly and bluntly to ignore any advice from any person about what is selling, what is hot, what you should write.

Write your own stories.

And if you do write your own stories, protect them from others, believe in them, and mail them to editors or get them up for readers to buy, you may be the next big thing and then thousands and thousands of writers will be trying to imitate you.

And they will fail, because there is only one of you.

Sacred Cow #8

YOU CAN'T MAKE A LIVING
WITH YOUR FICTION

This myth *"You can't make a living writing fiction"* is so clearly hogwash, I shouldn't have to include it as a chapter in this book. All anyone has to do is look at a certain fantasy writer in England being richer than the Queen. And the number of fiction writers on the Forbes List every year. And that's not counting all the writers publishing their sales numbers each month just from Kindle alone.

But, alas, new writers hear this myth all the time, constantly, from every direction, and sometimes from longer-term professional writers. It shouldn't be a myth at all, but it is.

Myth Origin

We have all seen the silly studies that an "average" fiction writer makes something like $2,345 per year. And, of course, people look at that and think, "Oh, my, no one can make any money writing fiction."

Of course, those who say that don't know how studies are taken, or what a number like that really means.

Most of the big studies ask every person who has a dream of someday writing a novel. The writers asked maybe have finished a few short stories, maybe even mailed a couple. They go to a writers' group regularly, and call themselves writers, because they are in the early days of learning their craft. They make no money. There are hundreds of thousands of this type of writer, all in the early days of learning.

Then, of course there are the writers who will never sell, a person with the best intentions, but no real drive to actually sell anything. Or if they do sell, it's to a small press that pays in copies or worse yet these days, they give their story away free to an online press and don't even get a copy.

Or they write poetry and are doing fantastic when they make a few hundred per year.

The studies ask all those writers how much they make, and the answer is almost always zero or not far above zero. Millions of "nothing" answers.

Then these studies include writers in organizations like SFWA, who lets a writer with three sales in the door. And Romance Writers, which has a huge chunk of membership that has never made a sale. All those thousands and thousands of unpublished or slightly published writers are included.

It's stunning to me that the average is so high, actually. But the truth is to get the final answer up to a few thousand, a lot of people have to be making a lot of money with their fiction writing to pull up all the beginning writers.

Writing, to my knowledge, is the only profession that takes studies this way.

It would be exactly like trying to figure out what an average lawyer makes by also including every undergraduate who is thinking of going to law school and every law student in the study about what they made working the law. Lawyers, in that type of study, would make less than two thousand average I'm betting.

Where Else Does This Myth Come From?

Duh? The answer is simple. It comes from all the people who are, for one reason or another, simply too afraid to try mailing out their fiction regularly to places who buy it. Or too afraid to put the stories up indie. Or only have one novel up and are wondering why they are not selling like Konrath. Or writers trapped in the agent myth, rewriting book after book for someone who wouldn't know what would sell if it slapped them.

For all those writers, it would be impossible to make a living at writing fiction. And thus, when you talk to them about making money, they are telling you the truth...

...From their viewpoint.

How about a writer who has sold three novels traditionally and for the first time understands how the money flows? Or has gotten five to ten stories up electronically. Those early writers are saying the same thing, of course. Selling one genre book a year is not enough to make a living writing. Putting up just a few books indie is not enough to make a living. Unless, you are fantastically lucky.

But most of us aren't that lucky, so a writer with one book a year, who has bought in to the writing-slow myth can't make a living, and they are telling other writers the truth as well...

...From their viewpoint.

So what about when you hear this myth spouted by a big name bestseller? I heard a New York Times bestseller in a keynote speech once tell 500 people there were only two hundred people in the nation making a living at fiction. Kris and I almost fell out of our chairs laughing, but we were just about the only people in the room laughing. Everyone else thought he was right. As it happens, I'm sitting next to him on a panel the very next hour, so as we were talking, I turned to him and said, "You know that 200 number is totally wrong."

He look sort of stunned and said, "That's what I had always heard." (The myth hits again and is repeated by big-name writer who is making millions.)

I said, "If that's the case, then don't you find it pretty amazing that there are seven of the two hundred on this one panel?"

He looked down the panel at the seven of us, all full-time fiction writers sitting on the panel. Then I asked the 100 people in the room how many were writers making at least $80,000 per year with their fiction writing. Five more people, two of whom I recognized, raised their hands. Twelve of us in the same room at a writers' convention. That stunned the keynote speaker, let me tell you, and we ended up spending the entire panel talking about this myth. And where that 200 number came from in the myth.

Turns out, there are about **200 NEW NAMES** on the major bestseller lists every year. (There are 780 yearly slots on the *New York Times* list alone, not counting the same number on *Publishers Weekly* lists, same number on the *Wall Street Journal* lists, and the 2,600 spots on the *USA Today* Bestseller list in a year.) So there are about 200 NEW NAMES in fiction hitting the bestseller lists every year that have never been there before. That's just the top spots. I'm not talking extended lists.

And of course, in this new world, I'm not talking about the growing number of novelists making a living indie publishing.

That number is growing by the day. But you get an idea where the silly idea of only 200 came from.

So, how many writers in the United States do make a living writing only fiction? Well, that depends on how you define "living." That's another shocker for me. For the longest time I figured over six figures gross per year was a living. At that level there are thousands and thousands of fiction writers making that much and a lot more.

But lately, I've been forced by discussions with other professional writers to look at reality a little bit more when it comes to "making a living."

A $2,000 mortgage, $1,000 for various insurance, $1,000 for various utilities, and $2,000 more for food and other details, like clothing, trips and such. $6,000 per month after taxes needed to survive. $72,000 per year, but if you are married and your spouse works, cut that number in half. Your half, to say you are making a living writing fiction only needs to be $38,000 per year. Slightly over $3,000 per month.

And many, many people I know make nice livings on less than that. A bunch less. So my number was way high when it came to "making a living" so I have no idea how many thousands and thousands and thousands of writers make a living.

It's a lot more than I even thought it was, to be honest.

How Do Fiction Writers Make Money?
(The Magic Bakery Metaphor)

Think of us (every writer) as a huge bakery and all we make are pies. Magic pies, that seem to just reform after we sell off (license) pieces of the pie to customers.

And each pie can be divided into thousands of pieces if we want.

The Magic Pie secret ingredient is called "Copyright."

Every story we write, every novel we write, is a magic pie full of copyright.

We can sell (license) parts of it to one publisher, other parts to another publisher, some parts to overseas markets, other parts to audio, or eBooks, or game companies, or Hollywood, or web publishers, and on and on and on. One professional writer I knew licensed over 100 different gaming rights to different places on one novel. He had a very sharp knife cutting that small section of his magic pie.

With indie publishing, most writers are only focused on one tiny aspect of their pies, the electronic rights. But interestingly enough, when a story or novel gets published electronically, it gets spread out to many, many stores, and sometimes other publishers see it and want to buy it for their project, or a movie producer sees it and options it, or a game designer sees it and makes an offer. So in this new world, getting stories up indie can help out other sales given time.

And indie published books are licensed in many other countries through Kindle and Kobo and iBooks. All different parts of the same pie.

And if you really understand copyright, you will understand those pieces are not even sold. They are simply licensed. But I am using "sold" for this article instead of "licensed" just because that's how most beginning writers think.

So each professional writer has this **Magic Bakery**, making magic pies that can be cut into as many pieces as we want and many of the pieces can return as if never taken, even after being sold (licensed) off. (You must learn copyright to really understand this... *The Copyright Handbook* out of Nolo Press would be a good start.)

Each Piece of the Pie Is a Cash Stream

And extending this metaphor just a little bit farther, you don't even have to have the same flavor of pie. Kris has Kristine Kathryn Rusch, Kris Nelscott, Kristine Grayson, Kris Rusch, Kristine Dexter, and others, not counting combining with me every-so-often as Kathryn Wesley or Sandy Schofield. And under her own name she writes articles, stories in all genres, and novels in many genres.

Each story, each novel is a pie. If you have a lot of product, you have a pretty consistent cash flow stream because you have so many cash flow streams working. (Think a bunch of small streams flowing together to form a river and you get the idea.)

Indie writers who are successful at this new world are saying this all the time. Joe Konrath constantly talks about getting up more work. I push writers to write more and more. And my *Smith's Monthly* is yet another way to blend a bunch of pies.

Indie writers are finally starting to see the advantage to having more and more product, more and more magic pies. Traditional publishers always did. They would have five or six new books per month per list, and they built those big buildings on lots and lots of small slices from many pies.

So, for you traditionally published writers, advances on novels are only one cash flow stream for a few pieces of a pie. That's why these days people say that hybrid writers, those who work both sides and all sides, are making the most money. See why?

Repeat: Each piece of the pie is a cash stream.

Let me try to explain this using just one piece of the pie.

Say you sold (licensed) the tiny piece of the pie called French Translation Rights, and your contract with the French publisher limited your book to trade paper only. (You could have also sold the piece of the pie that had French hardback rights, or French audio rights, or French mass market rights, or French film rights. You still have those in the pie and can sell them at any point as well. Get the idea?)

Your French publisher will have advances like your American publisher, and there will be royalties and so on. In other words, your French piece of the pie will flow money into your accounts just as your English novel sale does. And in this new world you don't need agents to sell these slices anymore. In fact, you'll sell them more often with just e-mail and direct contact.

And your German sale (license) would be the same. Your Russian. Your Italian. And so on and so on. Thousands and thousands of pieces of the magic pie can be licensed.

One more time: Each piece of the pie is a cash stream.

Say you went to ACX and put a story you had indie published into audio. Does using that one piece of the pie stop you from selling any other piece of the pie?

No.

And when the audio contract goes out of force, the audio rights piece of the pie suddenly appears back in your pie and you can license it again.

Magic!

You create the inventory, the pie, just once, but can license it for your entire life, having pieces you licensed keep coming back to the pie over and over, and your estate can keep taking and licensing parts of that pie for seventy years past your death. Nifty, huh?

Are you all starting to see why Kris and I are harping all the time about bad traditional publishing contracts? If you give too many rights to work away for too long, it never returns to your bakery to make you money. (Maybe in 35 years... again, study copyright.)

But Here Is the Problem Most Writers Face

A **Magic Bakery** owner who opens a shop and has only one new pie per year, only one flavor, has little chance of making enough money to make a living and keep his business open.

Just imagine (as a customer) walking into a mostly-empty store. You have a huge empty bakery that you have promoted everywhere, but you have only one pie on the shelf. All the rest of the shelves are empty.

Customer turns and leaves. (Would you trust a bakery with only one pie on the shelf?)

But imagine my store... I have shelves and shelves and shelves full of pies, walls full, twenty flavors, willing to do new flavors at any moment to customer demand, willing to license small slices of any pie at any time. I have a lot more chance of having a lot of customers and making a living than a store with only one or two pies.

When you step back and look at any retail store, what I am talking about is sort of basic business. I have inventory.

I have a crowded store and am making more inventory all the time to keep repeat customers happy.

Each piece of the pie is a cash stream. If I have four hundred pies in my shop, each with a thousand possible pieces, I have a huge inventory to make money from.

Each piece does not have to make me much money for it to add up.

Go back and look at my myth chapters about writing fast and about rewriting. See how it's all starting to fall together?

A Real Life Example:

One afternoon, while at a writers' retreat I wrote a short story called "In the Shade of the Slowboat Man." The story took me a few hours to write.

—Just a few hours to create that pie. It was rejected at the market I wrote it for, so I sold it to *F&SF Magazine.* Decent money.

—Then I sold another slice to the *Nebula Awards Anthology,* another small slice (nonexclusive anthology right) sold and then returned to the pie.

—Then I sold it to another reprint anthology (same right again), another small slice sold and returned to the pie magically for another person to buy.

—Then I sold the rights to an audio play made from the story, making more off of that slice than the other three before, and then I was hired with Kris to write the script from my story, so more money yet again.

—Now I have that story on Kindle, B&N, Sony, iBooks, Smashwords and other sites selling and making nice money each sale. And I have put it in a collection so it is making more that way each month as well.

I have made well over $10,000 income from one short story so far, and I still have the pie on my shelf in my **Magic Bakery,** still there for sale, even though it is selling electronically and in a paper version.

Say I decide to make a novel pie out of the story. Short story pie will remain and continue to make money, novel pie will be created and both will have thousands of slices to be sold.

I had Hollywood once give me $1,000 every six months for three years simply to give them the chance to buy a slice of one pie (story) on my shelf. That's right, I never SOLD anything from the pie. I simply said "Give me a thousand bucks every six months and I won't let anyone else buy that one small slice of that one pie."

They never touched the pie and I made six thousand bucks off of that option.

I love this business.

It Doesn't Take a Lot of Sales to Make a Living

Now understand, over thirty years I have published over 100 novels traditionally and hundreds of short stories. I have over 10 million copies of my books in print at last count a few years back. Yet many of you reading this have never read a single word of any book or story I have written. But somehow I have been making a living with my fiction for over 25 years now.

Why? Because I have a very full **Magic Bakery**, with a large number of pies to sell pieces from. You haven't read any of my fiction. Yet here I am, making a living with my **Magic Bakery**.

I sell one slice here, another slice there, a bunch of slices over here, and I keep selling them and the new stuff as well, over and over and over. I understand copyright completely, and I use that knowledge.

Can you make a living after writing only one or two novels and a few short stories?

The answer is no (without getting fantastically lucky).

You have a bakery with no inventory. An empty store.

You have nothing on your shelves. Nothing to really sell to customers, and even if they do buy a slice and decide they like your bakery and your goods, there is not much else for them to buy. So they won't come back. Duh.

But once you fill that **Magic Bakery**, once you have customers who know where to buy, know that your product is a good, quality product, then the money will come.

Each piece of the pie is a cash stream.

And a writer with a good inventory and the ability to sell the inventory to customers can make a large amount of money with fiction writing.

If I can do it, if I am one of the thousands and thousands of fiction writers making a living with our fiction writing, you can do it as well.

The Secret?

Just write, finish what you write, mail or publish what you write so someone can buy it. You know, Heinlein's Rules will build you one very nice **Magic Bakery** in a very short amount of time, actually.

And, oh, yeah, it's also a lot of fun.

Sacred Cow #9

TO BE GOOD, WRITING MUST BE HARD

This myth comes in many forms and has many faces, but let me put it as plainly as I can to start.

Myth: To be Good, Fiction Writing Must Be Hard. (And it can't be fun.)

Total hogwash, of course, yet it is stunning how many new fiction writers believe this, and how readers, when they bother to think about it, believe the myth as well. And, of course, almost everyone who teaches creative writing in a university program believes this as well, and teaches the myth.

Where Does This Myth Come From?

Answer: A thousand places, actually. But I think the best place to look first is at fiction writers themselves.

Fiction writers are people who sit alone in a room and make up stuff. By its very nature, one of the easiest tasks ever given to a human being. But, alas, fiction writers are people who make stuff up, and thus, making stuff up doesn't stop when our fingers leave the keys. We use words like "struggle" and "fought" in sentences describing the creation of a story. "I had to really struggle with that story." Or "I fought that story into existence."

Good, active writing. Who cares if the reality was you sat fairly still, in a comfortable chair, in a warm room, at a computer, and just made stuff up.

Don't forget that we fiction writers, by our nature, are drama queens, to say the least. Because our task is so easy and so much fun, we have to make it seem harder to those around us, and to ourselves, otherwise we get no credit for all the "hard work" we do every day.

Fiction writers play up this myth of "hard work" so much, we actually start believing it ourselves at times. If nothing else, fiction writers are the masters of self-delusion.

A second place to look for why this myth exists is the culture of publishing.

One manuscript page is about 250 words. This post is now a distance past that number of words right here. So if I write one page, 250 words, per day, I would be done writing in about 10-15 minutes. Sometimes quicker, sometimes longer. If I did that 10-15 minutes every day for one year, I would complete a 91,000 word novel, about a normal length paperback book.

Oh, yeah, that's hard work, sitting silently for 15 minutes per day and moving my fingers. And the current culture would consider me a prolific writer if I did that every year for ten years. Heaven forbid I actually write 30 minutes per day and produce two books a year.

We fiction writers have to really hide this math, and we have to really do a lot of drama to keep the world believing that working fifteen minutes a day typing is hard work. Stunning how good of a job we have done in this scam, isn't it? As I said, we are masters of delusion, self-delusion, and just flat making stuff up.

Of course, there is always the "art" argument that comes flying in. Fiction writers who want to hold onto the myth that writing is hard work talk a great deal about the "art" and the "craft" of what they do, especially out in public. And of course, see my rewriting chapters about that part of the myth. But the truth is, when we are really creating art, we are doing it from the back of our brains, typing fast, buried in the story.

Oh, wow, does this chapter make fiction writers angry at me. I pull out all their excuses and pull back the curtain. Sorry.

How Did This Start?

In the beginning (I love starting a sentence like that), all fiction writers struggled over simple sentences, meaning back in the early days of learning how to talk and write as kids, writing was hard for all of us. I went all the way through college avoiding any kind of class that forced me to do a paper or essay. I hated writing. It was just too hard. Much easier for me to do a multiple-choice test.

Most people never get past those early, almost basic memories. So we grow up thinking that someone who can write a story, an article, or heavens, an entire novel, have a special super power and are working really, really hard to write. Some selling writers I know actually still believe this.

And, of course, the pulp writers, pounding out thousands of words a day, actually were working physically hard on those manual typewriters. Go ahead, don't believe me, try pounding out a single page on a manual typewriter as fast as you can. You'll be covered in White Out and your arms will ache.

But sitting here in my perfect chair with perfect arm support, letting my fingers try to stay up with my old brain, I'm not doing much work. In fact, if I didn't get out and do some exercise, some sort of movement in the real world, I would turn into a 500 pound blob with fingers. I was headed that way about three years ago. Now I'm down to 199 and still losing and exercising. That's right, I have to get up and move away from the writing to do any real work or exercise.

Also, the early days of trying to learn how to tell stories is difficult and very frustrating. The people around you think you are wasting time, your family talks in worried whispers behind your back, your workshop hates everything you type, editors give you form rejections, and even your cat won't go near your computer chair. Everything about learning how to write stories in the early professional days is hard. No argument.

The early days of trying to learn how to write professional-level fiction is an ugly extension and reminder of learning to write as a child. Very basic fear. It's a wonder any of us ever learn how to write novels, now that I think about it.

And of course there's **Practice**.

Don't even mention that ugly word to fiction writers. Fiction writers, unlike any other brand of art, think they don't need to practice. However, early days of trying to get published (and make decent sales indie) forces practice on all of us. No one buys our practice sessions and calls us brilliant, so we keep putting out stories and novels until someone does buy one or we get more than family buying our books.

And this, of course, is one main problem with indie publishing. Practice. You practice and publish, but you should have no expectations. Hard to do. Easier back in the day when all you got were rejections for years. Putting your practice sessions up on Amazon and making no sales is harder to deal with. Not as clear cut.

Practice is hard work for the most part. Anyone who played a sport or a musical instrument knows this fact.

So when fiction writers are practicing in the early years, it is hard work.

Learning Is Uncomfortable by its Very Nature

When you are learning something new, it makes us all uneasy, makes us want to return to the status quo of not knowing something new.

We all like stability, but when learning fiction writing and the craft of storytelling, there is no stability. A fiction writer is constantly trying something new, constantly on edge, constantly learning, and thus it feels hard and uncomfortable for years at a time.

That's normal, just normal. And clearly not hard work, but because the learning and trying something new feels difficult, we think of it as hard work.

And this applies when we are struggling (nice word, huh?) through a story and it feels like it's not coming together. That, we say to other writers, is working. We had to "work" at the story, the plotting into an unknown place felt uncomfortable, therefore it felt hard and if it feels hard, it therefore must have been work.

As I said, fiction writers are great at self-delusion.

So the memory of working hard at writing still haunts all of us from our childhood. On my writing computer I have a novel to finish. But that feels like work, so I sit here at my internet computer, typing this instead. See, even I do it, still, after all the millions of words and over 100 plus traditionally published books.

So, as I do with every chapter in this book, let me try to outline in simple form where writing is actually hard, and where it isn't hard.

Where Writing Is Actually Hard

1) The business of fiction writing is hard.
No argument there at all. And that business comes flowing into the writing. Thoughts about selling or not selling stop most writers at times. That makes the typing hard. Just dealing with the myths around agents can drive a writer to a nap very quickly. To indie publish or not to indie publish? That can cause a writer to stop cold for months. Cash flow, doing proofs, doing covers, laying out books, and so on. Everything about the business is hard.

2) Discipline is hard.
Just carving out time to write fiction is hard. Really hard, actually. Especially in the early years when the feedback loop is so negative.

Simply finding time to get to the computer is hard when day job, kids, and bills get in the way. That's difficult for everyone and very hard work. The fun starts when you get to the chair with some time ahead, but getting there is hard work early on.

3) Writing more than six to eight hours a day is hard work.
I know, under novel deadlines, I have spent that many hours and many more at a computer. When you write for eight hours a day, you know you have physically worked at something. But fifteen minutes a day to write one novel a year. That's not work. Write ten thousand words a day for a couple of weeks and you will know real hard physical work in the area of writing.

Those are the only places I can think of that writing is actually difficult work.

Where Writing Is NOT Hard

1) Sitting in a chair for an hour or so a day, making up stuff, is not hard work.

It's just not. And no amount of whining or excuses from fiction writers will make me think any different.

2) Coming up with story ideas and novel ideas is not hard work.

In fact, after a while, professional fiction writers have far, far too many ideas to ever think about writing them all, and we are constantly coming up with new ideas every day. Coming up with story ideas actually becomes annoying because there are so many and it is so easy. (Fear of ideas not coming is something you learn your way past in the early days, the uncomfortable days. No worry. And if that scares you still, take the Ideas workshop.)

Where Writing Is Just Flat Fun

1) Sitting in a chair, making stuff up, while knowing that someone will pay you a lot of money for what you are making up.

Yup, that's fun.

2) Knowing that the typing you are doing today might still be read and earning you and your kids money seventy-five or more years from now.

No other job I know of has that wonderful aspect to it. That's fun.

3) Finishing and mailing or publishing stories is fun.

Some of you might call that work, the mailing process or the indie publishing process, but actually, it's fun. (If you think of it as hard work, if the fear is trying to stop you, you have other issues to get past.) Every time you mail something, or indie publish something, you are creating a potential, and that's exciting.

And these days, when you spend the time to learn how to put a book or story up electronically and/or publish it in paper yourself, you will discover that seeing that story sell two days after your wrote it or holding that paper book in your hand is nothing but fun.

As an attorney friend of mine once said, when he goes to work, he gets so much per hour and then goes home. When I go to work, finish a story and mail it or publish it, every day I have the chance of making a lot of money and being read by a lot of people and making money with what I did that day for decades to come. That's exciting and fun.

4) I wrote that!

Yup, that's fun, great deals of fun, simply saying to someone, "Yes, I wrote that." I can't begin to tell you how much fun it was a while back at a conference spending a good hour and a half signing books as fast as I could sign. I have an ego, just as anyone else, and trust me, that's fun. Signing books for fans who love your work is not work. It's an honor and a ton of fun.

5) The challenge of the business.

Nothing is easy about becoming and staying a professional fiction writer. The business, the push to continue, the dealing with money is never easy. But the challenge itself is great fun.

If you aren't the type of person that goes at something that seems impossible and says, "Oh, why not, let's try...," then you might want to find another job to chase. If you feel that security is everything in your life, then go work for Enron. That should do the trick. (Oh, wait, that company and all its pension funds are so long gone, and most people won't remember that name. I rest my case.) But if you love challenges, there is no more fun challenge than this business and making up stories.

Suggestions on How to Make Writing More Fun

1) Take the pressure off.

Simply put, this is not brain surgery. No life is in your hands other than some made-up characters. And you can kill them if you want, since you are God in your story. Take off the pressure.

2) Take stock of how you feel when you get up from a good writing session, where you finished pages.

Do you feel good, excited, happy? Most of us do, sort of like just coming off a good carnival ride. Remember that feeling when you go back to write the next session or the next day.

3) Make mailing manuscripts to editors or indie publishing them fun. Mailing and the game of trying to match the right manuscript with the right editor at the right magazine or house is fun. Frustrating at times, sure. But the more you make that part of things into just a game to keep as much writing on the market as you can, the more fun you will have and the less rejection will bother you. (If you are still mailing stories to agents, you really, really need to catch a clue.)

And indie publishing, for those of you who have not yet started because of fear, is just flat a joy. It has an uncomfortable learning curve, yes. But I would never be doing this crazy challenge and *Smith's Monthly* without indie publishing.

4) Stop calling your writing work.

Stop thinking of writing as a grind. Stop complaining to other writers all the time how bad the week was and how little you got done. Just stop.

In other words... **CHANGE YOUR ATTITUDE.**

If you have an extra ten minutes, write something. If you are lucky and have a few hours, be excited about sitting down and exploring whatever world you are running around in with the story. Come at the writing with excitement, with expectations of fun, with delight.

As a mug I use for tea says on the side, "Attitude is everything."

Over the years I have allowed myself to fall into some pretty nasty traps around the business of writing and writing itself.

I let myself forget how much fun it is.

I let myself believe that some writing was better than other types of writing.

I let myself think that it was better to not write than write.

I have managed to escape all the traps, but I was not immune to them by any means. Heck, I quit writing a half dozen times along the way.

That's right, I figured the grass was always greener on the other side of some fence, so off I went to start a comic book store, or off I went to play professional poker, or off I went to try to play professional golf for a second time. And every time, at some point fairly quickly on those side roads, I realized I had left what I loved to do, that I had left the easiest job on the planet, and a job that paid the most: Writing fiction.

I had left a job I really enjoyed.

So now I write fiction for a living once again, and I enjoy it even more than I ever did.

I sit alone, in a room, and make stuff up. That's my job description. I have, without a doubt, the easiest and best job in the world.

It is a giant myth that my job is hard work.

Sacred Cow #10

IF I DO (THIS OR THAT), I WILL KILL MY CAREER

This myth just gets more and more annoying by the day. So I figured it was time to take a hammer to the myth in this last chapter of this book.

If you catch some hints of annoyance on my part through this chapter, it's because I think this is flat out the stupidest myth there is. And one of the most dangerous because it causes writers to act in head-shakingly stupid ways. It also shows no understanding of the business of publishing, or the business of indie publishing. So please be patient with me. I'll try not to be grumpy.

If I Do "This or That," I Will Kill My Career

Now, of course, beginning writers are the ones saying this. You never hear long-term professionals like me or Kris or anyone else who has gotten a half dozen years making a living say this. Ever.

Why? Because we know it's just not possible. It really isn't.

Professional writers don't worry about mistakes killing careers, we worry about mistakes that will cost money or get us screwed or signing bad contracts or letting some agent rip us off.

Who can kill a career?

The writer who believes this myth can kill their own career simply by believing it. Sort of Zen, but true. Any writer that stops writing and just becomes an "author," (a person who has written) will kill their own career. *The writer stops writing.*

What is a "Career"?

My good old dictionary defines the term as "An occupation, a way of making a living."

I suppose by that definition it could be said I have a career. I write for a living, I sell books and stories. I helped start a new publishing company four years ago and now sell most of my stories to that company. And for years I was a part-time editor and still edit an occasional anthology. I have a reputation under this name and I have done so many things to this name, it's stunning the name is still alive, including telling people how fast I write and doing these Killing the Sacred Cow blogs.

Kris has many pen names. Do Kris Nelscott and Kristine Grayson and Kristine Dexter have careers? Or are they all part of Kristine Kathryn Rusch?

I think all pen names are just part of the career of the writer. But on the other side, it can be thought that each pen name has a career. Your choice how you look at it.

I find it wonderful that I can get the income from five or ten other careers (pen names). I did for years and years. That's a very cool thing about writing. Just like Evan Hunter got all the money from Ed McBain's career. Nifty how that works, huh?

And that writing under other names is just one thing that makes careers in writing impossible to destroy.

Why? Because even in the worst situations and after the worst mistakes, we can all just change our names and keep writing, that's why. Unlike any other profession, we are free to just be as many people as we want to be.

A business person tied to a resume can kill a career with a bad action or choice. An actor can kill a career because they are tied to their face. A doctor can make a mistake and kill a career by actually killing a patient.

A writer can decide to stop writing, which kills a writing career eventually. But again, that's self-inflicted.

But if the writer can clear out the ego and change names when sales drop or things go wrong, there is nothing to stop that writer from writing until the moment they die.

Writing careers can NOT be killed unless the writer stops writing.

Wait, let me say this one more time:

Writing careers can NOT be killed unless the writer stops writing.

But the belief that a career can be killed by a mistake is often terminal for a writer. This myth can be very dangerous if you believe it. The myth itself will cause you to stop writing and thus kill your own career.

Let me give a couple of main examples and some minor ones of how this myth rears its ugly head these days.

Mail a Novel to an Editor Against Guidelines

Yup, I know that all guidelines say "Agented Submissions." And for decades before that all guidelines said "No Unsolicited Manuscripts."

So? Who cares? (What are you all? Sheep?)

Editors need manuscripts, they are looking for good novels that they think will sell. And in this new world, agents will just get in your way and mostly they work for publishers. So why deal with them?

You send an editor a great few-page sample of your novel with a good cover letter, a short synopsis and a SASE and they will look at it. They might send you their form letter saying "get an agent." Fine, but they will look at it for the most part. And if you are close, the editor will write you a letter, and if your book is good and it fits, they will make you an offer on it. (Then you need to deal with an attorney and bad contract terms, but that's another topic.)

So, you all remember editors? The people who can buy books at publishing houses? Remember?

So sending a manuscript directly to an editor will not kill your career.

Why?

1) The editor won't remember your book if they didn't buy it.

I know many of you think you are the center of the universe, but honestly, the editors don't remember manuscripts or authors they don't read.

2) There is no such thing as a blacklist unless you threaten the editor with a gun.

3) Honestly, the editor can't come to your house and yell at you. Honestly, they just won't care if it doesn't fit their line.

4) The worst they can do is just toss your manuscript away and not respond, which some of the younger, rude editors do at times. You are out a few bucks postage. Shrug.

Yet I have heard hundreds of writers say "If I mail my book directly against guidelines to an editor, I will kill my career."

You won't!

But you might sell a book and actually start a career.

If I Indie Publish a Bad Story, I Will Kill My Career

I love this from new writers who think they actually know what makes a good story or a bad one. Of course they don't.

And to be honest, when it comes to my own stories, I don't know either. No writer is a good judge of his or her own work. None.

Any writer who thinks they are a good judge of their own work has far too much ego, or has spent far too much time in creative writing classes in college.

Professional writers can spot when another person's story works or doesn't work and why, but on our own stuff, we suck. Nature of how the brain works and again a topic for another post.

And indie publishing something really, really, really bad will not kill a career. No one will buy it. And thus not care.

Really is that simple.

You know... **Trust the readers**.

And if you are really afraid of a story, put it under a pen name (called a burner name) and don't tell anyone. Just let it sit there.

Publishing a story you think sucks won't kill your career!

It might make you a little money, however.

More Silly Thinking

Example... Kris got a letter the other day from a writer flat believing that if he self-published anything it would completely kill his career. Of course, he was a beginning writer, wasn't selling anything, and thus had no career. But he was convinced.

Example... I have heard many, many times from writers that if you don't have an agent, it will kill your career.

I haven't had an agent for eight years. I keep selling and making money. Interestingly enough, it's always beginning writers or someone with only one or two novels published that tell me this. We have talked about this myth already bunches of times in other comment sections, but it is always framed by "...if you don't have an agent, it will kill your career."

Truth: These days having an agent can do more damage to your income and long-term copyrights and income stream than not having one. Far, far more. Honest.

Example... I have received many letters over the last few years from writers afraid to negotiate contracts for fear it will kill their careers.

Kris and I have walked away from many, many contracts that had bad clauses that we just wouldn't sign and we negotiate everything and we still make our living at this business of fiction writing.

In fact, if all writers as a group suddenly grew a pair, we actually might get royalty rates for electronic publishing moved upward. But this fear of "killing a career" by negotiating a contract hurts us all.

And even worse, writers let agents do the negotiating, agents without legal degrees who can't practice law but do so anyway, and who are more concerned about keeping the publisher happy then helping the writer. Yeah, that gets us good clauses in contracts.

Any wonder contracts have been getting worse and worse over the last five years? It's all because writers are afraid of killing their careers. Most don't even have careers in the first place, because they aren't making a living at their fiction.

And why aren't they?

Because fear never gets you anywhere in business, folks.

I asked a few other professionals about other examples of where they hear this silly myth and I got hordes and hordes of stories, all funny to me and the other professionals, but all very real and believed by the young writers spouting the myth.

And these stories range all over the map.

Example... A writer who thought that if he didn't rewrite a manuscript at least ten times, he would kill his career. Hadn't sold anything yet for some reason. (grin)

Example... Another beginning writer was convinced that a bad cover on a book (he thought bad) would kill his career. His first novel from a traditional publisher and he thought he knew more than the art department in the publishing company and was trying to get another cover his friend drew to replace the cover. He did far more damage to his reputation than a hundred bad covers could have done. But he was convinced a bad cover would kill his career.

Not even that kind of stupidity would kill his career, but it didn't do him any good with that one publisher, that's for sure.

Folks, I have had more bad covers than I can count over the decades. I'm still making a living.

Example... Another writer swore that if he didn't have at least three people proof his story or novel before he indie published it, it would kill his career. He actually said he wanted his story perfect, to which the professional telling me the story laughed and said, "Yeah, as if there is ever a perfect story in publishing."

Summary

There is only one way for a writer to kill a career: **Stop writing**.

It really is that simple.

But if you go into everything you do in publishing believing the myth that you can make a mistake and kill your career, you will make all your decisions from a position of fear. And you will make horrid decisions.

And if you don't believe me on this, just ask any long-term professional writer, a writer who has been around for over twenty years, how many mistakes they have made. The professional will laugh and then more than likely ask which year? Or which dozen do you want first? Something like that.

And most beginning writers would tell me that writing a series like *Killing the Top Ten Sacred Cows of Publishing* would kill my career because I have said so many things that are against "common stupidity...I mean knowledge."

Hah, fooled you. I'm still here and selling and making a very nice living.

If you never stop writing, gain some courage, and stop worrying about killing your career, you might be stunned at what you can manage in this business. You will be writing and enjoying the writing until the day you die.

And that's a great reward.

So stop worrying and go have fun.

ABOUT THE AUTHOR

USA Today bestselling writer Dean Wesley Smith published more than a hundred novels in thirty years and hundreds of short stories across many genres.

He wrote a couple dozen *Star Trek* novels, the only two original *Men in Black* novels, Spider-Man and X-Men novels, plus novels set in gaming and television worlds. He wrote novels under dozens of pen names in the worlds of comic books and movies, including novelizations of a dozen films, from *The Final Fantasy* to *Steel* to *Rundown*.

He now writes his own original fiction under just the one name, Dean Wesley Smith. In addition to his upcoming novel releases, his monthly magazine called *Smith's Monthly* premiered October 1, 2013, filled entirely with his original novels and stories.

Dean also worked as an editor and publisher, first at Pulphouse Publishing, then for *VB Tech Journal,* then for Pocket Books. He now plays a role as an executive editor for the original anthology series *Fiction River.*

For more information go to www.deanwesleysmith.com, www.smithsmonthly.com or www.fictionriver.com.

The
WMG Writer's Guide
Series

*Think Like a Publisher 2014: A Step-By-Step Guide
to Publishing Your Own Books*

Killing the Top Ten Sacred Cows of Publishing

*Deal Breakers 2013:
Contract Terms Writers Should Avoid*

*The Pursuit of Perfection:
And How It Harms Writers*

*Surviving the Transition: How Writers Can Thrive
in the New World of Publishing*

Made in the USA
San Bernardino, CA
16 October 2015